# DANCING IN HIS
# PRESENCE

# DANCING IN HIS PRESENCE

## A GUIDE TO ESTABLISHING AND MAINTAINING A DANCE MINISTRY
### 2nd Edition

Margaret Brewington Wright, PhD

Library of Congress Control Number:            2013923341
ISBN:                Hardcover            978-1-4931-5644-3
                     Softcover            978-1-4931-5643-6
                     eBook                978-1-4931-5645-0

This book was printed in the United States of America.

Rev. date: 01/23/2015

**To order additional copies of this book, contact:**
Xlibris
1-888-795-4274
www.Xlibris.com
Orders@Xlibris.com
538280

# CONTENTS

# DEDICATION

This book is dedicated to the first visual and performing artist, my Lord and Savior Yeshua the Messiah, Jesus the Christ. He is indeed the author and finisher because "All things were made by Him; and without Him was not anything made that was made" (John 1:3).

# FOREWORD

All of a sudden it seems that every church has a "Dance Ministry." The problem is what I call "yawning and stretching." While I have a real appreciation for creative arts in ministry, it was always confusing to me to say the least, what qualified as dance ministry, liturgical dance, or otherwise. Many people, if they are honest, share my sentiments. The vagary and ill-styled writhing of the body that have been intended to creatively interpret and communicate God's love, care and invitation to meet Him more deeply have failed in many arenas of "dance ministry." That is, until now. Dr. Margaret Brewington Douglass-Wright has written a much to be admired and appreciated work that defines the breadth and scope of a movement. It is a methodology and prescription for dance ministry at its finest. Glorious in definition and inspirationally motivating, this work will assist any dance ministry to offer God their absolutely finest and best gift.

I have known Margaret for many years. Our history is rooted in our collegiate days as students at the University of North Carolina—Chapel Hill. I have had the privilege of watching her grow and develop into a powerful minister of the Word. She is a prophetic and gifted dancer—anointed to serve God's church with unusual dedication and unimaginable creativity! She is wonderfully talented and she has discovered the art of extending her gifts and talents to others through the pages of this book.

We owe Dr. Margaret Brewington Douglass-Wright an incredible debt of gratitude, for with this publication, many will find the wise counsel and instruction necessary to build a ministry that honors God and blesses people. You will appreciate the sound instruction inviting the dancer into a deep and personal relationship with Christ. You will also find the structural format for organizing and advancing the ministry, and for holding members accountable for their relationship to Christ and each other to be an indispensible guide for creating the kind of ministry that will exalt the Savior, edify the saints, and tear down the evil one's strongholds.

Dr. R. Neal Siler
First Shiloh Baptist Church
The Healing Place Center for Counseling and Spiritual Formation
Mechanicsville, Virginia

# ACKNOWLEDGEMENTS

Special thanks to all those who have gone before me and who have paved the way. Special thanks to the true "dancers of life": Alvin Miles and my spiritual daughter Cari-Lenn Orr for the front cover artistic depiction of the male "dancer of life" and my daughter, Tracey Turner for the original dancer and logo. I am grateful!

# FROM THE AUTHOR

"... in thy presence is the fullness of joy ..." Psalm 16:11

There is no greater joy in ministry than to experience the awesome presence of the Holy Spirit as you become fully engulfed in His presence. Dancing before the Lord is indeed an honor, a privilege and a joy. This book is by no means an exhaustive study but an illustrative one. My desire is to impart in you all that He has given me to impart and to encourage you to experience His fullness and completeness as you minister before the Lord in dance.

Study and learn how to establish a dance ministry that is pleasing unto the Lord. We want to present a ministry before Him that is pure "in spirit and in truth."

Allow the Holy Spirit to move you to a new level of "dancing in His presence."

.... The Author

# ABOUT THE BOOK

This guide to establishing and maintaining a dance ministry is a must read for Pastors, Church Leaders and Ministers of dance. Learn a biblical perspective on the art of worship through dance. Can anyone dance? What is the role of the worshipper through dance? What are the five critical safeguards in establishing a ministry? These practical guidelines provide keen insight into the biblical perspective and the establishment of the operational and administrative structure, vision, mission, budget, and the selection of dance movements, garments, and music for praise and worship.

If God leads you to begin a dance ministry, then learn the art of establishing a ministry that is holy and pleasing to the Lord by "dancing in His presence."

# CHAPTER 1

## Biblical Perspective: Is Dancing Scriptural?

### Eight Words for Dance In The Scriptures:

Yes! *God commands us* to praise Him in the dance. In Psalm 149:3 and Psalm 150:4, God makes a declarative statement concerning dance. He says to praise Him in the dance. He commands us to praise Him.

> Let them praise His name with the **dance**; Let them sing praises unto Him with the timbrel and the harp (Psalm 149:3, King James Version).

> Praise Him with the timbrel and **dance**; Praise Him with stringed instruments and organs! (Psalm 150:4)

**Interestingly enough, the Hebrew word for dance found in the both of these scriptures is Machowl.** Machowl originates from the word chuwl which means a round dance. A round dance can take on various meanings. It can be as simple as dancing around in a circle or as complicated as three dancers (or groups of dancers) performing the same series of movements in succession, each with a different beginning but merging at the end. Other examples, in the Old Testament, of the use of Machowl can be found in Jeremiah 31:4, 13; Lamentations. 5:15; Psalm 30:11.

**A second word for dance in the Old Testament is Chuwl, pronounced khool** (Judges 21:21, 23). This is my favorite of all the dance definitions. It takes away any excuse that we may give. Chuwl means to swirl or twist in a circular manner, to writhe with pain (especially during the process of giving birth) or to fear and tremble. Have you ever encountered someone who says that he or she cannot dance? Well, you ask, have you ever been in pain? Have you given birth? Have you ever responded to someone in fear? Well, then you were dancing and did not even know it.

**A third word for dance found in the Old Testament is Raquad,** **pronounced raw-kad'** (Job 21:11; Ecclesiastes 3:4; Isaiah 13:21; 1 Chronicles 15:29). This word for dance means to stamp about wildly or joyfully. An example can be found in David's joyful celebration of the entrance of the Ark of the Covenant. David, in 1 Chronicles 15:29, danced so wildly, stamping around joyfully, that he came out of his clothes and was rebuked by his wife for his "unkingly" behavior. In other words, David was "throwing down."

**A fourth word for dance found in the Old Testament is Karar,** **pronounced kaw-rar'** (2 Samuel 6:14, 16). Karar means to whirl while dancing. Whirl, as defined in the American Heritage Dictionary (2012), means to rotate or spin rapidly about a center or axis. It means to move rapidly in a circular manner in random directions. Furthermore, it can be defined as a state of mental confusion, giddiness, or dizziness. Just as in 1 Chronicles. 15, David danced before the Lord with all he had.

> David danced before the Lord with all his might; and David was girded with a linen ephod . . . And as the ark of the Lord came into the city of David, Michal Saul's daughter looked through a window, and saw King David leaping and dancing before the Lord; and she despised him in her heart (2 Samuel 6:14, 16).

David danced in such wild abandonment that he may have appeared to someone else from the outside (Michal) to be in a "state of mental confusion, giddiness, or dizziness." David knew the purpose of his dance, and he knew before whom He was dancing. Therefore, even his wife's open rebuke of his expression of love for his Father did not deter him. Instead, he responded to her, "And I will yet be **more vile [undignified]** than thus, and **will be base [humble] in** my own sight . . ." (2 Samuel 6:22a).

How about you? Are you concerned about your dignity? David did not let his title or anyone's perceptions of his way of worshipping God stop him. Instead, he demonstrated that he would yet praise Him. God's pleasure in David's form of worship, and his displeasure in Michal's rebuke are evident by God closing Michal's womb until she died. What is your excuse? Are you hindered by your title? Do you allow other people's perceptions of your worship hinder you from dancing in His presence? Will you "praise Him in the dance"?

**A fifth word for dance found in the Old Testament is Mechowlah, pronounced mekh-o-law** (Exodus 15:20; Exodus. 32:19; Judges 21:21; 1 Samuel 18:6; 1 Samuel 21:11; 1 Samuel 29:5; Jeremiah 31:4). Mechowlah means a dance company. In Exodus 15:20, we see an example of a dance troupe as Miriam, the prophetess, takes a timbrel (a percussive instrument) in her hand and celebrates the victory of the Red Sea crossing by leading a company of woman in dancing and singing.

Another example of Mechowlah, as a dance company, is found in Jeremiah 31:4. In this scripture, God talks of the restoration of Israel and says to His people that Israel shall be delivered, adorned with tabrets and shall go forth (in a dance company), making dances of happiness. As, exemplified in both examples, God acknowledges organized groups of dancers as well as the individual expressions of worship.

**A sixth word for dance found in the Old Testament is Chagag, pronounced khaw-gag'** (1 Samuel 30:16). Chagag means to march or move in a solemn procession or pageant. In this particular example, David's enemies, the Amalekites, were drinking, dancing, and rejoicing over the spoils taken from the land of the Philistines and the land of Judah.

**A seventh word for dance found in the New Testament is Orcheomai, pronounced or-kheh'-om-ahee** (Matthew 11:17; Matthew 14:6; Mark 6:22; Luke 7:32). Orcheomai means to dance in a row, a ring or in rank-like motion. In Matthew 11:17, Jesus uses an analogy. He compares the current generation's inability to respond to the truth to a group of children's inability to dance. Another example of Orcheomai occurs in Matthew 14:6 and Mark 6:22. Herod's daughter dances and pleases the king so much that he rewards her request for John the Baptist's head on a platter.

**An eighth word for dance found in the New Testament is Choros, pronounced khor-os** (Luke 15:25). Choros means a round dance or a dancing choir. Although similar to the Hebrew word Machowl, meaning a round dance, here we see another application. During the Greek era in theatre, a chorus or choros referred to a group of singer/dancers that appear onstage after the prologue, dancing in a ring or dancing while singing. According to Oscar Brockett in *History of the Theatre*, the chorus as a rule would enter the performance space in a stately march from several directions, either individually or in a group contributing to the effectiveness of the production through "movement, spectacle, song, dance" (p. 30). Most choral passages were sung and danced in unison or in an antiphonal response. An example of choros can be found in Luke 15:25, the parable of the prodigal son, as they celebrate the return of the younger son through a chorus of singers and dancers.

In the bible, there are examples of the enemy imitating and using dance for negative reasons (Exodus 32:19; Judges 21:21-23; Job 21:7-12; 1 Samuel 30:16; Matthew 14:6; Mark 6:22); yet, God commands us to praise Him in the dance (Psalm 149:3; Psalm150:4). Therefore, it is time (Ecclesiastes 3:4) for us to take back what the enemy has tried to use for his glory. It is time for God to arise and His enemies be scattered (Psalm 68:1). It is time for us to dance for God's glory!

Isn't it wonderful to know that God has made provisions for us in His Word to celebrate our love for Him through dance? Whether as an individual, in a company, in a rank-like file, in a circle, in a ring, in unison or in an antiphonal response, we can . . .

### *PRAISE HIS NAME IN THE DANCE!*

# CHAPTER 2

## Establishing And Maintaining A Dance Ministry

**Governance and Structural Guidelines:**

**How Do You Organize A Dance Ministry?**
**Steps to Organizing A Dance Ministry!**

1. **The first step in establishing a dance ministry is to fast and pray.**
   Fast and Pray! Fast and pray and get the mind of God for *your particular ministry at this particular time.* There are no two ministries alike, and there is an appointed season for all. Each ministry is confronted with different kinds of circumstances and is in a different stage of growth. Therefore, you need God's appointed plan for your appointed destiny. Erring from this truth may cause your ministry to stumble, miss its' designed purpose, or endure unwarranted persecution. If God leads you to begin a dance ministry, begin to inquire about the purpose, goals, structure and leadership of the ministry. God knows the plans He has for you. Once an individual approached me and asked me to assist her in establishing a dance ministry in her church. She was excited and thought the time was right. After giving her guidelines that needed to be established, I encouraged her to seek God. Later, she called and said that God told her not to go forth at that time. He said that the foundation needed to be established first. **Get God's mind for your congregation at this time. Do not try to open your own doors or copy others.**

2. **The second step in establishing a dance ministry is to build an intercessory team.**

## Building an Effective Dance Ministry through Intercession

Critical to the operation of an effective ministry is intercession. It is imperative that you have intercessors or that you link with an intercessory ministry. We wrestle not against flesh and blood but against principalities spiritual wickedness in heavenly places (Ephesians 6:12). Your battle is not against the dance member on your team or the leader in your church. We are not to war in the flesh (2 Corinthians 10:3), but to war in the spirit. For the Spirit makes intercession for the saints (Romans 8:26), speaking forth the mandates of God (Romans 8:27). Jesus Christ intercedes for us at the right hand of the Father (Romans 8:34). Therefore, we must intercede and through our prayers pull down strongholds (2 Corinthians 10: 4), and every high thing that exalts itself against the knowledge of God; we are to bring every thought captive through Christ (2 Corinthians 10: 5). We are more than conquerors through Christ (Romans 8:37). Therefore, when we intercede, we stand as ambassadors for Christ (2 Corinthians 5: 20), making intercession for all according to the will of God.

## Do not underestimate the power of the enemy.

As a ministry do not underestimate the power of the enemy to war against the Spirit through the flesh (1 Peter 5:8). The flesh may be yours or others. The results are the same. The enemy desires to bring enmity between the saints and God (Romans 8:7), saints and the sinners, and sinners and God. We are to be crucified with Christ, but live by the faith of the Son of God (Galatians 2:20), so that we can boldly say the Lord is our helper and we will fear not what the enemy or man can do to us (Hebrews 4:16; Hebrews 13:6).

## Be aware and beware of seducing spirits.

The enemy will send people to your ministry to thwart or hinder the move of God (Acts 16:16-18). Be spiritually discerning regarding who you allow in the ministry, who you place in leadership (Acts 13:1-3), and what type of activities you allow the dancers to engage in (Acts 13:3-5). The enemy will send people and opportunities your way (Acts 16:16-18), so if you are not judging everything by the Spirit (1 John 4:1-6), you will assume these people and events have been sent by God. Every ministry opportunity is not sent by God. Know by the Spirit when to go (Acts 11:11-14) and when not to go (Acts 16:5-7; Acts 21:3-5). Pray about everything (Ephesians 6:18; 1 Corinthians

14:15), and put your intercessors on the wall. I cannot emphasize enough the need to watch and pray! (1Peter 4:7; 2 Timothy 4:5).

## Do not underestimate the power of prayer.

I remember a time, when after several years of getting up at 5 A.M. to intercede, I began wonder if my praying did any good. After all, I did not always see the results. Of course, I had seen the Hand of God move during that time, but many times I had received only a witness in my spirit that it was done. Still at times, I prayed but wondered about the outcome. So, one day while praying I asked Him, "Father, does it do any good when I am praying." He did not speak then, but that night I had a dream. I dreamt that I was walking in a cave that was high up, in the top portion of a mountain. The cave had many caverns with openings all around. As I was weaving in and out of the caverns, I saw witches everywhere. The place was bustling with excitement as they were busy making plans and making items. Leaders were walking in and out among them, overseeing the process. I heard one of them say that when the horn sounded (blasted) they were to take flight, each going to his or her assignment. It was suppose to be a long, loud blast from the horn. I said to myself, I have to find some intercessors. I began running through the cave openings until I found about three people (Christians) in the back of the mountain in a cave. I told them, "We've got to pray." We began to intercede in the back portion of that mountain. The excitement and hustle and bustle of the witches continued, as they awaited their signal to leave.

All of a sudden, instead of a long loud blast of a horn, we heard "pop" "pop" "pop," like a fire cracker misfiring. Confusion set in. The witches began looking about hastily, bumping in to each other, appearing confused as to what to do. I said to the intercessors, "Let's get out of here" before they figured out we were there and what we had done. We rushed to the front of the cave opening and flew off over the tops of the next few mountains, away in the sky. When I awakened, I told the Lord that I would continue to intercede.

## Plan a Strategy for an Intercession Team!

Ask God for His strategy for His ministry. Once, while a member of a specific church, God began to put in my spirit His desire to birth ministries in that church. He asked me to meet with the Pastor to share what He had spoken to me. God had placed in my spirit to get a team of people to fast and pray weekly for the Pastor and ministry. So, I found three other people who were willing to pray. Each of us would fast one day a week until the Lord said to stop. We compiled a prayer list and prayed individually daily for the items on the list. Once a month, we came together as a team to pray. When I shared the strategy that the Lord had given me with the Pastor, he decided to join us; so, Monday through Friday, each of us had an assigned day to fast while all of us prayed. I would meet with the pastor periodically to update him and to receive from him any new areas of need. God kept us on this assignment for about five years. Not only did I see some ministries birthed in that church while I was there (dance, puppetry, and clown, etc.), one of our intercessory team members, who is still a member, has told me about the awesome things God continued to do after I left. GLORY TO GOD!!!!!!!

As intercessors, there are times God will cause us to stand in the gap for other ministries. Do it! God is faithful (Hebrews 10:23; 1 Thessalonians 5:24; 2 Thessalonians 3:3). He will not forget your good works (Hebrews 6:10-11), but will reward your work with results (1 John 5:14-15). **Pray and Watch God Miracle Moves!** God is faithful! Trust Him!

3. **The third step in establishing a dance ministry is to determine your vision, mission, and goals for the ministry, out of which will flow your governing and operational structure.** The vision, mission, and goals of the dance ministry should enhance the vision, mission, and goals of the church. Together, working as a team, the dance ministry helps the church to fulfill the calling God has for this body of believers. Remember, we are one body jointly fitted together, perfecting the saints for ministry and the evangelism of souls.

4. **The fourth step in establishing a dance ministry is critical to the success of the operation of the ministry: determine the governing structure and the operational guidelines for your particular ministry.** (See Appendix B.) There are a variety of administrative and spiritual leadership governing structures that may be used by utilizing the gifts that are in your congregation. If you are a pastor, you may want to approach a particular individual to whom you are led in your congregation to provide leadership for the dance ministry. This individual may serve as the director, facilitator, or choreographer of the ministry. He or she may be a person gifted in the area of administration. The person in charge of the ministry administratively does not have to be the choreographer. The choreographer may even be a youth member of your church, who works under the authority of an adult. Or, you may decide to use a team approach with a director and a choreographer. Be discerning regarding your selection. (See safeguards later in this chapter for guidelines.)

If you are a lay person who desires to start a dance ministry in your church and your pastor shares your vision for a dance ministry, consult your pastor about the governing structure and operational guidelines. It is important to know what he or she establishes for your ministry. For example, in one particular church setting, a sister consulted me about wanting to establish a dance ministry at her church. After our conversation, when she approached her pastor, he referred her to the Minister of Music. In this particular church, the dance ministry was organized under the authority of the Minister of Music. In others, the dance ministry may be directly under the Pastor or a Youth Pastor. Whatever the governing structure of your church, make sure you understand and follow the order set forth for your ministry.

If you are a lay person who desires to start a dance ministry in your church and the pastor does not share your vision for a dance ministry, respect the pastor and wait on the Lord to move. It is important to know God's timing. Do not move ahead of God. God is a God of order. If you are out of order, you will not have God's blessing. You will not have God's anointing.

5.  **The fifth step in establishing a dance ministry is generating guidelines for operation within the ministry which include:**

        a.   **Criteria for Participants in Dance Ministry**
        b.   **Selection Process**
        c.   **Rehearsal Process & Format**
        d.   **Technique Classes & Workshops**
        e.   **Five Critical Safeguards**

## Criteria for Participants in dance ministry

Construct a contract or memorandum of agreement that outlines clearly the criteria and expectations for the ministry. Establishing agreements on guidelines and expectations in the beginning helps to avoid confusion in the future. If you desire certain procedures for parental involvement (e.g. the drop off and pick up of the dancers, the observation of the rehearsal process), establish this clearly in your guidelines. Decide on a discipline policy for the participants in the ministry in the event someone breaks the rules. The policy will need to be clear and fair. Get the parent and child or the adult dancer to sign and date it, expressing an understanding. This establishment of a contract with guidelines helps to alleviate future dissension by making sure all persons involved know the requirements and expectations. Make sure you confer with the pastor or governing leadership in the establishment of these so that you will have his or her full support.

## Sample Criteria:

**Must be saved.** (Must have accepted Jesus Christ as Lord and Savior).

**Note:** Dance is a ministry. How can someone be expected to minister before the Lord on the behalf of others and he/she does not even know the Lord?

**Must be member of the church in good standing.** (Define criteria for "good standing.")

**Must be between the ages of___ and ___.**

**Must be a member of covenant care (cell) group** (if applicable).

**Note:** In one particular church, every member is assigned to a covenant care group. The covenant care meeting held once a month in the home of one of the Elders (Ministers), meets for a study of the Word of God, fellowship and food. It provides a more intimate setting for members (in a large congregation) to bond and grow. Therefore, in this church structure, the pastor required regular attendance to church and the covenant care group for all who desired to hold office or participate in a ministry.

**Must have previous training in dance.**

**Note:** Some ministries require previous dance training and will only accept dancers who are proficient. Other ministries provide training for all and accept all who are interested.

**Must have parental permission (if under 18 years of age).**

**Must be willing to get additional training.**

**Sample Contract or Memorandum of Agreement (See Appendix C):**

1. I understand that this is a dance ministry and not a dance performance.
2. I understand that everything will be done in agreement with the Word of God.
3. I understand that by joining I will be making a commitment to the ministry for one year; therefore, I will attend rehearsals and dance training classes.
4. I understand that I must conduct myself in a proper manner, and follow those in authority.
5. I understand that in order to minister in dance, I must attend all rehearsals.
6. I understand that if I must be absent from rehearsal, except in the case of emergency, I will contact in advance the necessary person (e.g. Minister _____ or Sister/Brother _____).
7. I understand that I must dress appropriately to minister.
8. I understand that if my schedule changes and I am unable to faithfully attend, I may request a leave of absence for a reasonable time period (if three months or more I may be asked to resign and reapply next year).
9. I have prayed (with parents and/or guardian, if applicable) and believe that God has called me to this ministry at this appointed time.

Participant Signature: _____ Date: _____

Parent/Guardian Signature: _____ Date: _____
(if applicable)

## Selection Process

In selecting and accepting dancers for dance ministry, establish clearly the criteria for selection. Some ministries accept everyone who is interested. Others require previous dance training or evidence of talent. Regardless of the decision, an established set of criteria for participation is still necessary. For instance, in one ministry, three levels of dancers were established: the company, the apprentices, and the youth dance team. Participants, ages 12 and up, may apply for the company and/or apprentice team. In order to be in the dance company in this ministry, a dancer must exhibit dance skills on Level II and above. This means that a dancer has to have training and/or natural ability equivalent to two years of formal dance training. In order to be in the apprentice program, participants must exhibit Level I ability. Level I is for a beginner or someone with talent who may or may not have had formal training. A dancer may move from one level to the next, as he or she progresses in skills. For example, as a dancer trains/participates in dance classes and dance workshops, he or she could accelerate his/her growth and thus advance from the apprentice program to the dance company in a period of months. The harder he or she works the faster he or she can climb. In this same ministry, the youth dance team is composed of boys and girls from the ages of five to 11. Although all dancers (the company, the apprentices, and the youth team) may minister together in any given setting, the level and degree of participation in the ministry differ.

Although this ministry has the three dance teams, there are opportunities for all church members to participate in corporate dance worship. For example, in a dance worship piece, all members of the congregation may be assigned various hand gestures or body movements. Or, in some situations special people in the congregation may be asked to wave a certain flag at a specific time in the service. Or perhaps, in a special children's program all children may be asked to participate. This is no different from the music ministry team. There are times when everyone in the congregation sings corporately in worship, but the praise and worship team should comprise people who are gifted in area of singing.

If your dance ministry requires previous dance training or evidence of talent for selecting and accepting dancers, use an assessment sheet with clearly established objectives in your tryouts or placement sessions (See Appendix D). This sample assessment sheet may be used for determining all levels of placement, as well as, indicating areas of needed growth when planning future training workshops. Tailor it to your needs or craft your own set of criteria. The key is to make it specific to what you are looking for so that all will know what you expect. If your ministry accepts all who are interested, then you may not need this form.

## Rehearsal Process and Format

1.  **Schedule/plan time wisely and adequately.**
    Do not over schedule your rehearsal time. Do not waste time. Use the time wisely. It is better to have few rehearsals and work hard than to have many rehearsals and work lightly. Three to four hours is sufficient in most cases for a rehearsal period. Some ministries meet weekly for a determined period of time. Others meet on an "as needed" basis. Make sure the schedule you select for your ministry meets your needs. Too many rehearsals will cause the dancers to become weary and, as a result, may produce a problem with attendance. I know of one particular dance ministry that meets weekly. Unless the teams minister weekly, you may find the demands of this schedule too great. Usually, what happens in this case is that it becomes difficult to get 100% participation, consistently. As a result, it can become a waste of time to choreograph sections with missing members. It is better to have fewer

rehearsals with everyone there than many rehearsals with few there. Break the choreography into sections, and pinpoint the teaching sections for each rehearsal period. Avoid meeting extra times for dancers who did not honor the attendance policy. This may cause resentment among those who honored the commitment of time. Avoid the temptation of allowing the dance rehearsal to become a social hour. The dancers will resent the misuse of their time and may begin to miss rehearsals. Plan timed scheduled breaks, and stick to the amount of time specified. Start on time. End on time. It builds your credibility.

2. **Give calendars for rehearsals, technique classes, and dates for ministry.**
Planning in advance allows others to plan in advance. This is an invaluable in assuring a good turnout in rehearsals/classes and ministry. It will save you countless hours of redoing choreographing.

3. **Devise a means of remembering choreographing.**
You may use dance notation with symbols, pictures or word phrases to help you remember. Videotaping sessions is invaluable. Make sure you get written permission from all participants (and parents of minors) before recording, and make sure you use the tape for the specified purpose only (privacy issue).

4. **Establish a rehearsal format is consistent:**

____Play praise and worship music when the dancers enter. (You may want to go early to intercede or conduct spiritual warfare prior to the dancers' arrival.)
____Teach about worship and praise (five minute nuggets). This is invaluable in training ministers of dance.
____Spend time in prayer and praise. This reinforces the need for a private devotional life and allows you an opportunity to teach by example.
____Prepare a method and plan for teaching so that it is clear who is in authority.
____Provide breaks and refreshments (if possible and/ or necessary), but guard your time.

# Suggested Rehearsal Format

- ❖ Prayer of Cleansing
- ❖ Praise and Worship and Prayer (includes five-minute nugget)
- ❖ Warm-up Period
- ❖ Introduce Choreography and Concept
- ❖ Review

❖ Cool Down
❖ End it with a Prayer

## Technique Classes and Workshops

### Provide training in dance.

You may want to set up classes weekly, biweekly, or monthly. If you are not skilled in teaching dance technique, you may want to refer your dancers to an outside dance instructor to teach technique, if no one in the congregation is trained to teach others. Or, you may want to bring in a dance technique instructor for workshops (See safeguards).

Suggested Technique Format (Lockhart, 1977):

_ _Warm-up
_ _Developmental section of the lesson
_ _Presentation of new technique
_ _Movement combinations (axial and locomotor)
_Presentation of the problem-use improvisational experiences related to the problem
_ _Presentation of solution of problems
_ _Locomotor movement ending with a return to center
_ _Cool-down period

# Five Critical Safeguards

1. *Do not confuse ministry with performance.*
   In the secular dance studio, in a culminating event the objective is to present a recital, a finished product, for all to see the technique mastered. In ministry through dance, our desire is to not to demonstrate technique through a "finished product," but to usher in the presence of the Lord that He might finish the work in these "these products," namely us.

2. *Do not confuse anointing with technique.*
   Often, dance ministries will bring in someone to conduct dance workshops and do not know them that labor among them (1 Thes. 5:12). The individual(s) may be technically correct, but may not offer spiritual substance. In his book, *Ministry of Helps and Church Administration,* Bishop Burton emphasizes the importance of having someone with the anointing. You can dance technically correct to pleasing audiences and cheering crowds, yet exact no change upon the people. It is the anointing that promotes healing and produces fruit.

3. *Do not under estimate the need for leadership with spiritual discernment.*
   There may be an opportunity to bring in someone to assist with the ministry who is not a "blood bought" Christian, or someone who has not confessed Jesus Christ as their Savior, so be careful of the spirit that is being imparted into your dance members. Once, while working in a secular setting, I brought in a choreographer. During the process of the class, I began to see the manifestation of something God had spoken to me during my quiet time that morning. He had said to me that the choreographer had stated that in this dance "you are welcoming elders into the city, but actually you are ushering in demon spirits. Watch today as your dancers begin to get sick." Sure enough, on that particular day, as the guest artist began to teach the class, one of my dancers came up to me and said, "Mrs. Douglass, I don't feel well." Shortly thereafter, another one stopped dancing and approached me saying the same thing. I, instantly, halted the class and struck that dance from our repertoire. I want you to understand that I had been a Christian for a long time. This was not a "Christian" setting. It was acceptable, by design, to bring in someone of this person's caliber to teach a dance class. It had been done before in many settings. But you see, I had begun to get close to the Lord and had asked Him to give me a discerning of spirits. If this can occur in a secular setting, how much more should we guard our spiritual little ones. Know them that labor among you! (1 Thessalonians 5:12)

4. ***Do not confuse talent with maturity.***

   Often, in the church setting we are mesmerized by talent. We can confuse talent with anointing, and we can confuse talent with maturity. It is not uncommon to feature and highlight those that demonstrate a skill that all can see is excellent. As in the case with many churches, these are the people who are sometimes placed in leadership over a particular area. In his book, *Ministry of Helps* and *Church Administration,* Bishop Burton establishes criteria for selecting the right person, at the right time, and warns against an erroneous selection. It takes special leadership to administrate all the various components of the ministry. Do not underestimate the enemy's ability to attack leadership. You may be placing someone in a position who is not mentally and spiritually mature enough to handle the spiritual responsibility. Then, you wonder why things go so awry.

5. ***Do not confuse confidence with conceit.***

   Sometimes, we can get so confident in our dance ability that we do not see the need for additional training and workshops. Imagine a minister of the gospel saying, "I do not need to learn anymore."

## Attire For Rehearsal and Ministry

**Modesty is the key.** Everything should be done decently and in order. In rehearsal and in ministry you want to ensure that the dancers are well supported and covered properly.

### In rehearsal:

**Female:** Should wear garments that cover the body appropriately but provide ease of movement. Clothing should be made of natural fibers that absorb sweat and allow the body to breathe (Smith, 1991). Leggings, such as tights and/or stretch pants, keep the muscles warm longer and aide in the prevention of injury. A good support bra should be worn by anyone with a breast size over 32A, in order to avoid tearing the underlying structure of the breast (Penrod and Plastino, 1980). Ordinarily, leotard tops are desirable in a technique class; it allows the dance instructor the ability to see the alignment in your body. It may be necessary for persons with certain body types to wear a top that is a little looser. Remember the key is modesty. Use wisdom and good judgment.

**Male:** Should wear garments that cover the body appropriately but provide ease of movement. Clothing should be made of natural fibers that absorb sweat and allow the body to breathe (Smith, 1991). Dance belts are essential for the male dancer to ensure ample support and guard against ruptures (Penrod and Plastino, 1980). A one-piece dance belt worn under the clothes gives more support than the athletic supporter (jock strap).

## In ministry:

**Female:** May begin, initially, with a basic white outfit (a dress or a white round skirt and white blouse combination.) The skirt generally is composed of eight to 11 yards in order to create the fullness necessary for beauty and choreography. For example, while executing turns and using the wing expansions in certain dance movements, the added fabric creates a nice visual effect. This outfit can be used in conjunction with assorted vests, sashes, overlays, and banners to cover the bodice and waist and to create several different outfits. Matching palazzo pants underneath the dresses and skirts are needed for modesty purposes.

**Male:** May want to select dark or white pants as basic with a white shirt. It can be dressed with sash and banner. Robes, vests, military uniforms, suits of armor and other garments mat be added or used as the dance dictates.

## Additional General Guidelines:

1.  **Be creative with patterns.** May select assorted patterns and use a combination thereof for an outfit, if you have a seamstress in your ministry that can sew well, or if you contract with someone outside the church, if necessary. One particular dress that I use quite frequently is a combination of three patterns, the sleeves are from a bridal pattern, the bodice from a dress pattern, and the skirt from the circle skit pattern. Use your creativity in adding adornments: tassels, ribbons, stones, etc.
    **Note:** Garments designs become the property of those who design them. Do not copy any design without the expressed permission of the designer. If I were you, I would get it in writing. Keep a record of your own designs, and date them.

2.  **Select outfits that are appropriate for the music, movement, and purpose** (e.g. worship, praise, and celebration, ceremonial).

3.  **Make sure you can move in the outfit with ease.** Some patterned designs and fabrics are beautiful to the eye but are a nightmare for movement. Make

sure you can lift your arms, turn, or change levels with safety and freedom. If you are not free to move, you will be preoccupied with your clothes and encumbered while dancing.

4. **Select appropriate shoes in color and style for the purpose and choreography of the dance.**
   Flesh colored shoes and hose are available on special order from some dance stores. Jazz, ballet, tap and character shoes may be necessary, depending upon the dance. Dancers may go barefoot, if acceptable in the congregation and the event. (You may want to dance barefoot only in dance areas that you know are clean of bacteria and hazardous items). Be careful about dancing in socks and other shoes not specifically designed for dance. It makes the bottom of the foot slippery on certain surfaces and could cause injury.

5. **Secure hair away from the face to avoid injury.** You need to be able to see without distractions when turning or bowing. While turning your hair could cover your eyes; and consequently, you or someone else could get hurt.

6. **Remove jewelry unless appropriate for the particular dance piece.** The jewelry may reflect the light and can produce a glare. (Please respect the married dancers; however, who do not want to take off their wedding rings.)

7. **Remove colored nail polish.** It creates uniformity and avoids distraction.
8. **Select makeup that blends and establishes uniformity with the group.** Makeup is needed especially when ministering in a large setting. It helps to avoid a washout look under the lights. In some cases, participants may be able to wear the same shade of lipstick and blush.

9. **Avoid any clothes that draw attention to the body.** Our goal is to draw them to the Lord.

## Music Selection:

**Select music that edifies the spirit.** Kevin Conner in *The Tabernacle of David* (1976) explains that the "type of music" affects the dancing. He warns of dancing that is "associated with sensuality and immorality" (p. 261). Music with these qualities leads to dancing with these qualities. Our *purpose* for dancing is to *usher in the presence of the Lord*; therefore, our *music should usher in the presence of the Lord*. Personally, I only select music for choreography that moves me to dance in His presence.

**Select music that is appropriate for the occasion.** The music selection directly affects the purpose of your dance. If the purpose of the service is seasonal or thematic, then you want to select music that fits with the season or theme. Adherence to this suggested guideline can help to create a flow of unity in the service.

**Select music that is appropriate for the age of the audience and the age of the ministers in the dance.** Children respond better while listening to music and participating in teaching that are presented on their level. Equally so, dance and music will capture the minds of the youth, if there is a connection to the piece. Young adults and mature adults may prefer another style of music. Proper assessment of your audience and dancers can make for a successful ministry presentation.

**Select music that is appropriate for the time in the service.** Music helps to establish mood. If I am ministering in the beginning of a service, I tend to select music that is more lively (outer court). If I am ministering directly before the spoken Word, then I tend to select a worship piece (holy of holies).

**Select music that produces a worship experience not a "party atmosphere."** David Frazier, in *Send For Me A Minstrel*, warns of the danger of music glorifying self rather than God. This book brought to mind a dream I had in 1970's. In the dream, the world was filled with hysteria and pandemonium as people were running in the streets, trying to find safety and shelter. It was the end times; I was running through a neighborhood, looking for a church. I finally found one and hastily ran into the sanctuary. As I entered, I discovered a host of people in the pulpit and choir area, jamming. Abruptly, they all stopped and turned to look at me. Being uncomfortable with their stares, I stammered, "I was trying to find God." The crowd glared at me in disbelief, roared with laughter, and turned to continue their jamming session. Slowly and despondingly, I lowered my head and walked out of the church.

**Ask the Lord for wisdom in selecting your music.** He knows the congregation. He knows the purpose that He wants to accomplish (Proverbs 3:6).

# Floor Selection and Care:

One of the most sensitive areas for dance ministry is the floor space on which one must minister. Ideally, dancers should never dance on very hard surfaces, such as concrete (Smith, 1991). Jumping and leaping on hard surfaces jars the joints and causes damage to the knees, back and internal organs. Carpet softens the blows somewhat, but does not prohibit the jarring. Instead, you should dance on a sprung floor, varnished or covered with linoleum. Unfortunately, in many church sanctuaries and fellowship halls, dancers are exposed to such hard surfaces. If your church is in the process of building and renovating, pastors should consult with the contractors about the proper surfaces to ensure that the areas for ministry in dance are safe areas for your ministers of dance.

## Budget Concerns and Considerations

**The initial cost in the start up of a dance ministry will vary**.

The initial cost should include attire, music, and training. Generally, most churches use their facility for rehearsal and dance workshops, thus, cutting out the cost of renting a space. Music is needed, but generally supplied by the church's music ministry. If funds are needed for securing music, then this amount will be included in the budget. Most churches allow the ministers in dance to use the CD/recording equipment present on site. A portable CD/iPod/iphone/tape player may be needed, if other methods of the playing music are not available, or if the ministering team will minister in a park or a nontraditional setting. These items can be borrowed from the church or another ministry, if the need is there, and if the money is not available. Some ministries invest in a video recorder for choreography and filming ministry events.

**The cost for dance attire (garment, shoes, and accessories) generally fluctuates, depending on the place of purchase, the amount of purchase, and the type of fabric.**

It is sometimes better to travel a distance or shop online to receive a greater discount, if you are buying large quantities. Some stores in New York, or other places, will make items available through shipping. This may be beneficial, if items can be brought wholesale, or if they can be purchased in large quantities. Generally, an entire outfit of dress, culottes, tights, and shoes can cost as much as $200 or more per dancer. Some ministries require the dancers to purchase their own garments. Other ministries assist in paying portions of the cost. In one particular church ministry, the church purchased the fabric for all outfits; however, the dancers paid for shoes, tights, and sewing cost. Due to the cost of the entire attire, this ministry generally gets one new outfit per year.

**Negotiate with the local vendors.**

You are a valued customer and you are producing revenue. Those that know me know that I will bargain.

**Training is essential.**

Whether, a dance consultant is brought in, or the dance ministry team is sent out, additional training is imperative!

**\*Proposed Sample Yearly Budget**

## ZINA CHRISTIAN CENTER DANCE & BANNER MINISTRY

Space rental for rehearsal...............................................................$0
Equipment (portable CD/iPod) ....................................................$500
Music (CD/ tapes/ recordings)......................................................$300
Mailings ...........................................................................................$100
Garments...........................................................................................$1000
Sets/Props (candles, fabric, banners, etc.).................................$500
Training for leaders or dance members .....................................$1000
Video/ Camera film .......................................................................$300
Books and study materials.............................................................$500
Publicity, ads, and posters.............................................................$200
Team travel expenses (conferences & workshops)........................$1000
Total..................................................................................................$5400

**\*This is a merely a sample budget. It can be adjusted to suit your needs and your ministry.**

# CHAPTER 3

## Developing A Technique for Worship: Do's and Don'ts . . .

### Developing a Technique for Worship:

First of all, I cannot stress enough the importance of proper alignment in the execution of dance movements. Technique is imperative to ensure proper alignment. James Penrod and Janice Gudde Plastino in *The Dancer Prepares* warns that "faulty placement will weaken and injure you if you repeat it often enough." Establishing physical control helps to avoid injury and promotes the mastery of movement. Training in dance technique promotes proper alignment and helps to ensure the control in the execution of dance movements. Make it a critical part of your dance training.

### Is there a biblical basis for movement?

**Yes. You can derive sources for movement from the biblical meaning of words:** For instance, there are seven Hebrew words of Praise: Yadah, Towdah, Halah, Shabach, Barak, Zamar and Tehilla. Each of these words denotes some form of movement. These Hebrew words and definitions of movements can be incorporated in dance choreography. For example, when choreographing a dance for the song, "We've Come to Worship Him," we investigated the meanings of the words for worship in Hebrew and Greek. We discovered that Hebrew for Worship was Shachah shaw-khaw (7812 Genesis-Jeremiah) [1] Prostrate-reflex in homage to royalty. Likewise, the Greek definition for worship is proskuneo (4352) [2], which means "to make obeisance, do reverence to" (from pros, "towards" and kuneo, "to kiss"). The word signifies an act of homage or reverence. Each of these words phrases can be used to create dance phrases. Therefore, we chose the meaning of both words to create dance phrases and explored various forms of lying prostrate, reflexing and bowing and created a worship piece.

In another example of the use of a biblical word, if we were to select "karar," we would select lively music and choreograph a dance phrase with jumps, leaps, spins and turns. Although, there is nothing written that says that you have to use definitions, I find that it can be a wonderful beginning.

**Yes, You can derive sources for movement from biblical postures:** In keeping with the above exploration of worship, I can find examples of "postures" used for worship. For instance, in 2 Chronicles 20:18, we see the placing of the face to the earth, as an act of humility and worship. This movement, in conjunction with a transitional movement of lowering the dancer to the floor, I would incorporate the placing of the face to the earth in a transitional phrase; and then shift the dancer to another position, perhaps kneeling. These sets of movements can be used to create a dance phrase. Another example of the use of biblical posture can be found in Psalm 95:6, where we are encouraged to worship by bowing down. Experimentation with various ways bowing can produce another set of movements for choreography.

## What are some additional sources of movements?

## Sign Language

Sign language can be used as a stimulus for choreography. Whether the signs are used in their pure form or elaborated through hand gestures and body movements, it can be a beautiful expression of praise and worship. On one occasion, we began a dance piece with one dancer walking out in the dance space and signing the first verse of the song. The same signs were then elaborated through movement by a group of dancers and transposed into dance phrases. The combination of the signs and the sign dancing was breathtakingly beautiful. **Note: Make sure your signs are accurate.** You do not want to offend. I remember attending a program one time where the children had been taught to sign a song by an inexperienced teacher. The children were smiling brightly but signing incorrectly. After the concert, during our conversation, I was very disturbed to find out that the teacher had tried to teach herself signing from a book. She had confused some of the signs by not understanding the directions given. Although, it was a "hearing" audience and most did not understand sign language, I was grieved to know that the teacher did not teach the children to say what she thought they were saying. She did not take time to get training or to consult an expert.

## Natural Gestures

Natural gestures can be another source of movement. Observations of the natural walk, run, leap, sitting, and rising can be used as choreography by the dancers. Natural gestures of the arms, hands, and face can also be included, as well. Observe the movements of a baby and the ease of movement. These resources for movements are a natural part of our everyday life and can be used to create a dance.

## Visual Art Work

Visual Art can be invaluable asset in dance composition. The symmetry and asymmetry in a picture's design can help to produce a wonderful tableau for the stage, as well as, provide a starting or ending position for a dance.

## Genres of Dance

Dance movements from various genres inclusive of ballet, modern, African, Israeli, tap, clogging, hip hop, folk etc. can be used in choreography. Care should be given in selecting movements to ensure that the meaning of the movement is in keeping with the message of the music and the occasion. It is imperative to have a discerning person to work with the dance ministry, as well as, other ministries in the church. We do not want to offend the Lord and those we are trying to draw. All movements may not be acceptable for all situations. Please be mindful, however, that some people may refuse certain dance movements from some genres because of their own prejudices and not by the leading of the Spirit. If you are uncertain about using a specific movement, then leave it out. God says that His sheep can hear His voice and know Him (John 3:1-5). He is able to speak to you to give you directions. Are you listening?

> **General Note: Avoid movements that draw attention to the body and tantalize the flesh. Rule of thumb . . . "If in doubt . . . Leave it out!!" In everything you do, do it all to the glory and honor of God!**

1    taken from *Abingdon's Strong's Exhaustive Concordance Of The Bible.*
2    taken from *Vine's Complete Expository*

# CHAPTER 4

# The Role of a Worshiper
# Through DANCE

**God desires that we worship Him in "spirit and in truth" (John 4:21, 23-24).**

Worship in Hebrew from Genesis to Jeremiah is Shachah shaw-khaw (7812)[1]. Shachah means to prostrate oneself or stretch out face down-reflex (lower the body) as in the homage to royalty. In the New Testament in John 4: 21, 23-24, the Greek word for worship, Proskuneo, means to reverence, fall on your face, or to kiss like a dog licking his master's hands. In other words whether Hebrew or Greek, God desires that you reverence Him, make obeisance to Him, kiss Him, reflex in homage to Him, and bow face down before Him in "spirit and in truth." If you research "spirit" and "truth," you will find that the Greek word for spirit means pnuema (wind, spirit, life) and the Greek word for truth it means verity (real, straightforward), not concealing. In other words, God desires that you worship Him with your very breath and life giving Him the glory due Him, presenting your real self before Him, in spirit and truth.

## In order to worship Him in spirit and in truth, I must know Him.

As a minister of the gospel through dance, I must know Him. God desires that we know who He is. God says in Jeremiah 9:23-24, " . . . let not the wise man glory in his wisdom . . . let him glory in this that he understandeth and knoweth me . . ." God desires that we know Him. If we do not know Him, how can we effectively tell others about Him? If we do not know Him, how can we come boldly to the throne of grace? How can I lead others into the presence of the Lord when I do not go and have not been there?

## My mission as a worshiper in dance is to first enter into His presence and second to usher in others.

### First, I must enter into His Presence.

I must have my personal established time of praise and worship with the Lord. I must know Him, intimately, as my Savior and my Lord. I must be sanctified by the shedding of Jesus' blood and the washing of the Word. If I do not know Him, how can I draw others? I tell the Lord, repeatedly, Father, "one thing I desire [of You] and that will I seek after, that I may dwell in [Your] house all the days of my life, to behold [Your] beauty and to enquire in [Your] temple" (Psalm 27:4). I want you to know You. I want Your very breath on my face. I want that "mouth to mouth" and "face to face" relationship (Exodus 33:11). I want You to exhale, so that I can inhale. I don't want to be like the children of Israel, who knew Your acts. I want to be like Moses. I want to know Your ways (Psalm 103:7). When we know someone's ways, it implies a more intimate relationship. It suggests that we have spent time in their presence studying and fellowshipping with them. Anyone can tell you what you did after you have done it. If I truly know you, I can determine what you will do before you do it.

I remember an experience I had over the Christmas holidays. My sister, my father, and I had gone to a nearby track to walk. After circling the track a couple of times, my father began lagging far behind us. I told my sister, "Watch Daddy! He is going to go under that tree over there for shade." Sure enough, as we rounded the curve, we saw my dad casually ease under the tree. After a few minutes of walking my sister said, "I am going to ask Daddy to go and get us some water." "He is not going to go," I replied, "He is going to say that he will give you the car keys and that you can go and get it." Sure enough, as we circled the track again, my sister asked, "Daddy, will you get us some water?" He replied, "Naaaaw, I won't get you the water, but you can use my keys to my car and go get it." My sister knew his acts; I knew his ways.

### Second, I must usher others into His presence.

I must allow the Holy Spirit to minister to the congregation by ushering them into His presence, leaving them there, and allowing Him to minister to their needs. My desire is to get so engulfed in the presence of the Lord that I am with Him and Him alone.

I remember an experience that I had while ministering one time in Virginia. My prayer was, as always, "Lord, I want to dance the way I do at home, when no one is watching." On this particular occasion, I felt the power of God surge through me like never before. I could not even feel my feet touch the floor. I was ministering a piece called, "Healing In His Wings." The Lord instructed me to go through the audience and touch certain people. Later, that night, my roommate in the hotel told me, "Girl, when you came out in the audience, you looked like an angel. When you went by, people were slain in the Spirit." To Be God The Glory! To Be God The Glory!!!

It is my desire that God touch you. It is my desire, as He ministers through me, that the power of God will so engulf me that the overflow will cause people to healed, delivered, and set free (Isaiah 61:1-4). In order to do this, I must have a personal relationship with Him. I must yield to His Spirit and obey Him.

**I MUST KNOW HIM.** I must be saved, clean, delivered, appointed and anointed. I must be a true worshiper of Him, worshiping Him in spirit and in truth, not hiding my real self.

**There is no greater joy than ministering unto the Lord and having His Spirit engulf you! Oh what a foretaste of glory divine!!!**

## What are your personal motives for being a part of the dance ministry?

What is your purpose for dancing? What is your goal? Bishop Burton in his book, *Managing God's Finances* (1999), explains how one's motives for serving affects one's attitude. So, what is your motive for being a part of a dance ministry? Is it to be seen of men? Is it to parade around in a cute outfit? Is it to hang out with your friends? I know of one incident, while directing a dance ministry, when a parent withdrew his daughter from participating. Later, he approached me and explained that he had pulled out his daughter because he found out that she had joined only to be with her friends. I really admire and respect this brother. How many parents would have done that? When you minister in praise and worship through dance, you wage war on the enemy's kingdom. The enemy is not going to sit by and do nothing. The Word says the enemy comes "to kill, and to steal, and to destroy" (John 10:10). He is going to attack. If your motives for dancing (being on the front line) are wrong, you will faint in the midst of adversity, or you will be a casualty. What are your motives? (1 Corinthians 3:13).

1.  Taken from *Abingdon's Strong's Exhaustive Concordance Of The Bible.*
2.  Taken from *Vine's Complete Expository*

# CHAPTER 5

# Choreographing the Dance: Praise and Worship

**"Dance is a visual art that uses the dancer's body to create architectural designs in space."____ Penrod and Plastino (1980)**

Dance is a visual art. It is imparted in the recipients through the natural eye. The moving and inclusion of certain elements of dance can ensure that the final picture (architectural design) is a picture worth remembering.

## Elements of Dance and Dance Concept

The craft of designing and shaping dance involves the use of the following elements: time, space, energy, and shapes (Minton, 1986). A dancer moves through space (personal space or general) executing shapes (curved, angular) using varying degrees of energy (sustained, percussive, vibratory, swinging, suspended, and collapsing) at varying tempos (slow, sustained). The patterns created by the movements and postures help to shape the concept or the idea of the choreography or dance. For instance, in the dance piece, "We've come to Worship Him," we decided that the central idea, theme or concept of the piece would be worship. In determining the beginning picture we wanted to create in the minds of the congregation, we explored the various postures for worship and decided to open with a proscenium picture of four individuals worshiping the King on various levels, in various shapes, throughout the stage space in varying degrees. One stood, one kneeled, one bowed and one lay prostrate. Although this is a simplified example of such a complex process, it demonstrates how even as the dance begins, the choreographer can help create a picture in the congregation's mind by using levels and shapes to portray the meaning of the dance.

## Choreography Rehearsal Process: Create, Impart, Perfect, Minister

### Creating the Concepts and Movements

One method of creating choreography is through improvisation. Improvisation (making it up as you move) can be used in many ways. One way of using improvisation, when dealing with dancers who are comfortable moving and who are not intimidated by others in the room, is to play the piece of music you have selected; allow each dancer to move freely as inspired. Watching the dancers move and/or recording this exploration period can inspire new dance phrases that can be used in the current dance as well as future dances.

Dancers, who are not comfortable with moving or intimidated by others in the room, are more hesitant to improvise. Therefore, these dancers may benefit from additional directions. For instance, in the dance piece, "We've Come to Worship," while in our improvisational phase, I selected six words and wrote them on individual slips of paper: respect, honor, love, adore, worship, and revere. Each dancer was given one slip of paper (with one word on it) and told to find an area of the room to work where he or she would not be disturbed. In that space, each was to create a sixteen-count dance phrase using that word as inspiration. What does that word mean? How would you show the meaning through your body movements? In other words, each had to count from one to 16 while moving (creating a picture that described the word) and had to remember the movements created. After each dancer explored and created his or her sixteen count phrase, we came back together as a group and watched each person perform his or her dance phrase. It was so beautiful to see the similarities as well as the differences in each choice of expressing worship. These individuals' phrases were explored, extended, and developed to create the dance. The piece remains one of my favorites.

### Imparting the Concepts and Movements

This step can challenge your teaching ability. How do you impart (teach) that which you (the choreographer) desire to see (your dance concept) on others (the dancers)?

One way to begin is to break your dance movements in sequences, then introduce the first section of the sequence to the dancers. **Dancers will vary in their rate of learning; therefore, be flexible.**

For instance, some dancers are microwaves, some ovens, and some crock pots.

## Microwave Dancers

**Some dancers (Microwave Dancers) are quick to learn a dance phrase and quick to perfect it.** These dancers usually feel comfortable with improvisation and may be used to create phrases for the next section, while the others are still working to learn the first phrase given. Later, when you divide the dancers into groups to practice, these microwave dancers may be able to serve as peer tutors. Try them! A great deal depends on their temperament. Sometimes, they may learn quickly from you, but may not know how to teach others choreography that is easy for them. Since the ability to teach (impart) can vary from the individual to individual, use wisdom when assigning partners or asking one dancer to teach another. (See the following.)

## Oven Dancers

**Some dancers (Oven Dancers) are quick to get the sequence of the phrase, but need repetition in rehearsal in order to perfect it.** Although, repetition may be a part of the rehearsal process, dancers should be encouraged to continue to perfect (rehearse) the dance phrase outside the rehearsal process as well. Some of the oven dancers may be able to serve as peer tutors. Again, a great deal depends on their temperament and their ability to teach others. Use wisdom!

## Crock Pot Dancers

**Some dancers (Crock Pot Dancers) are slow to grasp the phrase and need overnight or longer to process it.** These dancers learn at a slower pace, but "Man, oh, man, it is delicious when they finish." The seasoning has filtered all the way through. Please, be sensitive to how each person learns. Encourage each dancer to learn at his or her own pace. Simplify steps or movements when necessary or assign different steps or movements to different dancers. Remember, we are one body jointly fitted together (Eph. 4:16).

**Assign partners for practice.** This allows individual dancers an opportunity to get feedback from a peer and to practice in a small group setting. Make sure when partnering that at least one of the individuals feels confident with the movement phrase. Otherwise, monitor them closely and provide assistance.

**Determine how much time you will give them to work together.** Monitor the time and process by walking among the groups. You may need to assist at times, when you see the need. Remember teaching is a form of rehearsing and rehearsing is a form of teaching.

## Perfecting the Concepts and Movements:

After you have selected the key dance phrases and music for your ministry's presentation, you can begin to shape or put together the dance piece. Through rearrangement of the movements, a dance phrase may change directions (same, contrast), move to a new level (high, medium low), or vary in timing (regular time, half time, double time), in order to create your designed effect. As a result of changing the direction, level, shape, and timing your final project may be combinations of solos, duets, trios, or whole group dance phrases all in one dance.

**Some common methods of choreographing phrases are in the following forms: AB, ABA, round, theme and variation, canon, and narrative.** (For the purposes of discussion, we will use an eight-count phrase as our main dance phrase.)

**AB**-If I have an eight-count phrase and develop a series of movements using it, I can term that first section A. If I choreograph a contrast or a different series of movements for another eight-count phrase, I can name this new section B. Thus, by combining the first section (A) and adding the section (B), my new dance phrase is a sixteen-count phrase called AB. This phrase can be used in several places throughout the dance.

**ABA**-Similar to the technique above in choreographing the AB sixteen-count dance phrase, I can add a repeat of first section A at the end of B to create a new section of twenty-four counts called ABA. Therefore, after I perform AB and add A, I have create a new dance phrase, ABA.

**Round**-The round dance is similar to the singing of the "round" song, "Row, Row, Row Your Boat." In the round dance, two or more dancers dance the exact sets of movements (ABC.), and may continue indefinitely, but with each dancer beginning at a different time and ending at a different time. As a result, as they dance, different parts of the dance phrase coincide but may never dance the same part of the phrase at the same time. For instance, if there are three groups similar to the round song, group one will begin first with groups two and three joining in, respectively. Group one will finish first, then group two and finally group three.

**Canon**-A canon is similar to a round dance with the exception of the ending. At the end of the canon, the dancers join in dancing the same final phrase, at the same. The round dance is a simple form of a canon.

**Theme and Variation**-The dancer performs theme and then a variation of the theme. For instance, a dance may perform A (an eight-count theme) and then in succession perform a variation of the same theme or set of movements adding on new movements each time A is repeated.

**Narrative**-The dancer tells a story through movement. Although props, scenery, sound effects and stage lighting are not necessary, they may used to help tell the story.

# Ministering the Concepts and Movements
# Selection and Progression

## The Selection

**Use wisdom in selecting the dance movements for the congregations.** Assess your audience. Ask the Lord to give you wisdom. If you are visiting another church, you may want to check with leadership about the spiritual maturity and acceptance level of the church members. I remember, once, one of my spiritual moms asked me to join her while ministering on the coast of North Carolina. She was speaking and wanted me to minister in dance. Originally, we were to minister to one fellowship group. While there, an opportunity opened for us to minister at a second church. Before we appeared before the second congregation, my spiritual mom pulled me aside and told me that the church was very traditional and would not receive dance but would receive hand gestures. So, for this ministry opportunity, I danced with my hands. God still moved!

**Make sure you choreograph movements on the level of your dancers.** Assess your dancers. In selecting your dance movements for choreography, be sure to assess the levels of your dancers. It can be very frustrating for both dancers and choreographers when the movements selected exceed the ability levels of the dancers.

## The Progression:

**The progression or order of the program is very important when ministering several dances in one service.** Discern the time of day and the occasion. In order to effectively lead the congregants from the Outer Court into the Holy of Holies, from the cares of the day or world to a mindset for worship, a certain order may be essential. Therefore, you may want to start with a lively, upbeat dance (outer court) and gradually move to slower ones (Inner Court and Holy of Holies). Remember, you are dealing with people from different walks of life and with different types of personalities. If the program is in the evening, you may be ministering to people who have just gotten off work, or who are preoccupied with the cares of the day. Therefore, in order for all to reach the place of unity in worship, you may have to "prime the pump." A well planned progression or order of dances can set the atmosphere for worship.

**Set the tone with prayer and take available opportunities to teach the congregation.** Prior to the service, prayer is essential to charge the atmosphere for the worship experience. Be sensitive to the Spirit of God throughout the worship experience, following His lead and taking opportunities if they arise. During one ministry event, the sound system began to fail. As the church staff worked to correct the problem, the Lord led me to lead the congregants in prayer and worship, using the experience to teach about spiritual warfare. Be open! Be ready! Be prepared!

## Progression Purpose

The following progressive chart identifies some objectives, movements and suggestions of music you may find helpful:

### Outer Court

**Objective:** Helps congregation to shake off worldly cares.
**Movements:** Allegro, quick, lively, vibrant___ clapping, hoping, jumping, leaping, spinning, etc. Sometimes, you can incorporate congregational participation through gross motor movements.
**Music:** Praise

### Inner Court

**Objective:** Prepares the congregation for worship
**Movements:** Smooth gestures and slower deliberate movements with more control
**Music:** Praise

## Holy of Holies
**Objective:** Brings congregation to a still, receptive mode so that the Holy Spirit can speak, strengthen, heal, move, restore, and deliver__ Expect the Spirit to speak.
**Movements:** Adagio, slow__ soft, deliberate gestures and movements, at times complete stillness.
**Music:** Worship

**Sample Program progression:**
**AN EVENING OF PRAISE AND WORSHIP**
(This is an actual ministry event held at First Congregational United Church of Christ, Raleigh North Carolina.)

## Outer Court
**Dancers:** children (ages: two to eight)
**Music:** "Let the Spirit Rise Within Me," Donut Man
**Movements:** Allegro, quick, lively, vibrant___ clapping, hoping, jumping, leaping, spinning, etc.

## Inner Court
**Dancers:** children (ages: two to eight)
**Music:** "With All My Heart," Donut Man
**Movements:** Smooth gestures and slower deliberate movements with more control

## Outer Court
**Dancers:** Youth, Teens and Adults
**Music:** "O Sifuni Mungu," First Call
**Movements:** Allegro, quick, lively, vibrant___ clapping, hoping, jumping, leaping, spinning, etc.

**Dancers:** Congregation participation (Transitional piece in program so soloist could get ready)
**Music:** "O She Ba Ba," Danibelle Hall
**Movements:** Hand gestures

## Inner Court:
**Dancers:** Adult soloist (Transitional piece in program so dancers could get ready)
**Music:** "Friend of Wounded Heart," Brooklyn Tabernacle Choir
**Movements:** Symbolic gestures/Interpretive dance with smooth gestures and slower deliberate movements with more control

**Dancers:** Youth, Teens and Adults
**Music:** "Anointing Fall on Me," Ron Kenoly
**Movements:** Rank-like file, hand gestures, circles, changes in directions and levels

**Holy of Holies:** (This is a closure piece to bring in all other dancers.)
**Dancers:** All ages
**Music:** "All honor, All glory, All power to Him," Ron Kenoly
**Movements:** Rank-like file, hand gestures, candle placement dance, changes in levels and directions

## Other Choreographic Considerations:

**Setting:** Make sure the place is set properly for worshipping through dance. If you can have special needs, (e.g. furniture to be moved, props pre-set at a certain time in a certain place), be sure to assign someone (a stage manager, dancer or assistant) to move the items and to ensure that this task is done. Practice, prior to the time of the ministry, so that everything will flow smoothly and timely.

**Sound:** Sound effects may be used in lieu of and/or in conjunction with music.

**Lights:** Effective lighting can be added during the ministry in dance, especially if it requires special lighting effects: spotlights, candles, dimmed lights. Again, practice, prior to the time of the ministry, so that everything will flow smoothly and timely. Assign specific people.

**Props:** Props may or may not be used. The type of dance and the purpose of the dance will determine this. Use props to enhance movements and create a visual effect (picture ideas): crosses, candles, banners, streamers, etc. Do not be afraid to experiment. Make sure you practice with the placement and the execution of the props before ministry time. Determine where they will need to be set, so that you can grab them and return them with ease and without distraction, when necessary.

**Garments:** See section on attire.

## Choreographic Proccess
## Rehearsal: My Process

**My first step in designing choreography is to fast and pray.** I remind the Lord that it is His dance piece and ask Him what He would like to see. Then, after I have fasted for a determined period of time, I begin to work. If I am the choreographer for a group, I will ask the entire group to fast. If I am working with children, I seek wisdom. Usually, I and the other leaders fast.

**Second, I will be the first to admit that I am a process oriented choreographer and a visual learner.** These two combinations mean that I love to create the choreography with the dancers and to see the design of the dance unfold as I shape it. Often, I enter the rehearsal space with a concept and few dance phrases. I am very clear as to the overall effect that I want to achieve, but I have to experiment with improvisation in order to get it. This method of the choreography has its advantages and disadvantages.

### Advantages:

One advantage is that the dancers help to create the piece; therefore, they can remember the movements and sequences better. A second advantage is that this method of choreographing allows me as the choreographer an opportunity to modify/shape the movements to specific individuals. For instance, I may have a certain idea in mind for my dancers, but when I see them execute it, I may have to modify or adjust the movements to the ability levels of the dancers or to the physical space so that it works. I tell my dancers to relax; they will look good in the end!! Smile!

### Disadvantages:

One disadvantage is that this method is time consuming. It is much faster to walk in the rehearsal with the dance already choreographed/created and just teach the steps to the dancers. The second disadvantage to my method is that it drives the sequential learner crazy. The sequential learner desires everything in a set order and has a difficult time changing steps when you have taught the movements out of sequence. I try to compensate for this type of learner by giving an overview of the piece and telling them how each section will connect. I, also, try to make it clear when we are just exploring movements, so he or she will not set the movement to memory and become frustrated if I change it.

## Choreographic Proccess
## Rehearsal: An Alternate Method

A friend of mine has a different approach to choreography. She gets on her face before the Lord and does not get up until He shows her every move. This works best for her.

Determine the best way for you, and be flexible. Sometimes you may have to change from your usual way of choreographing because of the circumstances. For instance, one time, when we were ministering two dances at a conference, I told the Lord that I did not have time to do it my way. I fasted until God gave me peace, and then I went to bed. That night, in a dream, I saw the entire dance. I arose quickly, rushed to get paper and pen. I drew pictures, made notations, and wrote word phrases to help me remember. Boy, were my dancers surprised when I walked in the rehearsal with the dance already choreographed. By the way, that dance has always been one of my favorite pieces.

## Choreography Copyrights And Respect

### A valuable lesson

Learn about copyrights and intellectual property. In order to use someone else's choreography you should ask permission and give the proper credit in the program. Some choreographers place their dances on YouTube or DVDs for public use. In this case, it may have been released to public domain. Other choreographers require that in order to use it, you have to gain permission and then give credit in the program. Learn the difference and be respectful! **I thought I would pass this on!!**

# CHAPTER 6

## Can Anyone Dance?

**Yes! Yes! Emphatically, yes.** God commands us to praise Him in the dance (Psalm 149:3; Psalm 150:4). If you recall, one of the Hebrew words for dance is *chuwl*.[1] As stated earlier, one of the definitions for *chuwl* is to writhe with pain or fear; therefore, whenever someone says he or she cannot dance, quizzically I ask, "have you ever been in pain?" It is my contention that if you have ever writhed with pain or fear then you are capable of dancing before the Lord.

**How do I get started ministering before the Lord through dance?**

1.  Know Him as Savior and Lord (Romans 10:13).
2.  Allow Him to baptize you in His Holy Spirit (John 20:21).
3.  Establish a regular quiet time with Him to seek His face (Psalm 27:4).
4.  Plan a period of praise and worship (John 4:24).

## Follow guidelines set below, if you need assistance:

**Well, first, you must know Him as Savior and Lord.** If you have never accepted Jesus Christ as your personal Savior then, now is the time. The bible says, "If we confess our sins, He is faithful and just to forgive us our sins, and to cleanse us from all unrighteousness" (1 John 1:9). "All we like sheep have gone stray . . . every one of his own way, and the Lord hath laid on him (Jesus, Yeshua) the iniquity of us all. (Isaiah 53:6), Jesus Christ's blood was shed for your sins. Do you believe that Jesus Christ, Yeshua the Messiah, is the son of God? Do you believe that He died for your sins? Then, accept His sacrifice or atonement for your sin. Please allow Him to come into your heart, today. If you come to Him, He "will in no wise cast you out" (John 6:37).

## Just pray the following:

Father, I come to you in the name of Jesus. I admit that I am sinner. I have blown it. I don't know you as my Savior and Lord. I want to know you. I believe that Jesus Christ is the Son of God. I believe that He died on the cross for my sins and that if I confess and repent of my sins, you will forgive me. I ask that you to forgive me for my sin and cleanse me from all unrighteousness. I desire to have you in my life, in my heart. Come in. I give you an open door. Change me; cleanse me; deliver me; and set me free. Thank you for a new life in Christ. Thank you for saving me, redeeming me, cleansing me, and setting me free. **Amen!**

**If you really meant that prayer . . . HALLELUJAH! YOU ARE A BLOOD BOUGHT CHILD OF THE KING!!!**

If you have prayed this prayer for the first time, let me, your pastor, or someone in leadership at your church know. If you are not a part of a local church, please connect with a local church that preaches the uncompromised Word of God and tell the pastor of your decision.

**Second, allow Him to baptize you in his Holy Spirit** (Acts 19:2; Roman15:16). I believe that the time is now and has come that "they that worship Him **must** worship Him in spirit and in truth." I believe God is saying "whosoever will, let him come." I believe that God is taking the church to a new level of praise and worship. I believe that those who walk with Him, intimately, are going to see miraculous manifestations of God, even angelic visitations. But if you do not know Him, you will not be able to experience this new level. If you are not in tune with His Spirit, you will be like the five foolish virgins, left behind.

God is a spirit; therefore, in order to commune with Him we must commune through our spirit. I know you may have been touched by God, but now it is time to be infilled by God. If you have never been baptized in the Holy Ghost and now want to be . . .

## Just pray the following:

Father God, I desire to experience Your fullness. I desire to experience Your completeness. I desire to be baptized in Your Spirit. I renounce all works of darkness and refuse any involvement of Satan in my life. Satan, I no longer belong to you. Take your hands off God's property. I choose to be transformed by the renewing of my mind. Father, infill me with Your Spirit. In the name of Jesus, I pray. **Amen.**

Now, take in a breath and "receive ye the Holy Ghost" (John 20:21). Allow Him to permeate your body, spirit, and soul. The Word says, "If ye then, being evil, know how to give good gifts unto your children, how much more shall your heavenly Father give the Holy Spirit to them that ask Him?" (Luke 11:13). Thank God for His gift of love. Thank Him for the gift of His of His Spirit. Now spend time worshiping before Him.

**Third, establish a regular quiet time with Him face to face (Psalm 27:4).**

God desires that you intimately fellowship with Him. He desires a "mouth to mouth," "face to face" relationship with you. You were created for His pleasure (Revelation 4:11). You were created for His pleasure!!! It is in His Presence that you receive the fullness of your joy (Psalm 16:11). So, establish a quiet time today that will give Him pleasure and you joy.

**Fourth, plan a period of praise and worship (John 4:23).**

Yes. Yes. Yes! Paul said he would pray in the spirit and pray with the understanding; he would sing in the spirit and sing with His understanding. Paul was acknowledging that sometimes his prayers and songs were initiated through the unction of the Holy Spirit, and at other times he would initiate praying and singing with his understanding. I would like to parallel that experience with dancing. I can dance initiated through the unction of the Holy Spirit, and at other times I can dance initiated with my understanding.

Plan a period of praise and worship. Begin to include dance as a part of your daily worship in your quiet time with the Lord. Create a daily log of experiences (**See Appendix E**). You will be amazed by all that unfolds in your relationship with Him as you "dance in His presence."

# Here is a suggested starting point.

If you ask know how I can get started since I am not one of those "Let it all hang loose people," then follow the suggested starting point guidelines.

**First, pray a prayer of cleansing**. Confess all sin that would hinder you from coming before the Lord.

**Next, begin to praise Him for whom He is.** Call Him by His name(s). Express your love to Him. One of my favorite things to do is to have what I call "spiritual pillow-snuggle talk" with the Lord. I begin calling Him by all His names that I know from the Word of God, e.g. Jehovah Jireh, Rose of Sharon, Alpha and Omega, etc. Then, I call Him love names I know in the natural, e.g. precious, love, etc. Then, I move in the spiritual realm and struggle with Him nose to nose and call Him love names as unctioned by the Spirit.

**Next, I begin to dance with Him.** If you have never slow dragged with the King of Kings, you are missing a treat. Yes, He can even dip. If you are not ready for this level of spontaneous intimacy, take one of the Hebrew or Greek words for dance mentioned in chapter one. Read the definition. Tell the Lord that you want to dance this way in His presence today. Put on music, and begin to incorporate those movements in your worship. Use the diary form (**See Appendix E)** to create a record of your time of worship. You will be amazed!

If following these instructions seem kind of awkward, or if it feels weird going through a physical action to obtain a purpose, then recall when you were in elementary school. You were taught to raise your hand before you spoke, so that the teacher could call on you. You were told to line up in order to go to lunch or outside for Physical Education (P. E.). In the post office and bank you follow the ropes set as guidelines for the lines, as you wait to be served. So don't say it feels weird going through a physical action to obtain a purpose. You do it all the time.

If you are a person that freely moves and do not need any directions concerning lifting your arms, swinging your legs, spinning, leaping, jumping, bowing, and laying prostrate, then ignore the above instructions; do your thing; worship the Lord, and get busy dancing!!!

## Now the excuses:

**I am too fat.** Well, I had an experience that really shook my world. I want you to know that the devil does not play fair. I had always been very small all my life, until an injury occurred. Due to an injury, initially and later emotional distress, I jumped from a size eight to squeezing into a size sixteen. When you move from an eight to a sixteen within three years, don't you know that it messes with your mind? Come on, now. And you are a dancer? Well, needless to say, it troubled me so much that when the Lord told me to step out and start making dance videos I stumbled. I said, "Lord, I can't. I already look fat and the camera adds ten pounds. I don't need to look fatter. I struggled with that thing. I struggled with whether to continue to dance. Now, you may shrug it off, but for me it was devastating. It was hard enough dealing with the comments from my relatives and friends, but to put it on video . . . please.

Well, I began to say, Margaret, how are you going to encourage others to dance if you don't do it? How can you tell people who are considered fat (plus size) they have no excuse if you use it as one? For Whom are you dancing?

I decided to step out! I decided that I was going to continue dancing. I was going to do what God had called me to do. If someone had an issue with my size, then that was his or her issue. I was going to obey my King. As a result, during a ministry event as I ministered in dance at a conference there was a lady (an older, heavier lady) that kept watching me. As I left the pulpit area, she grabbed my hand and said that she was blessed, but she looked at me in astonishment and said, "And you are so agile." I chuckled to myself, as I walked away.

**I am too old.** Well, I am a grandmother and great-grand mother. My father, at seventy-seven, still tended his garden and was active in the community and the church. My aunt Ada, as she neared one hundred, tended a garden with me. Well, she tended it; and I handed her the hoe. Ummm . . .

**I have no energy.** Well, grab some barley green and sulphured molasses, and let's go!!

**I have never had dance training or I don't know how to dance.** Well, get some training and learn how. Anyone can dance and anyone can get training. Remember the question "have you ever been in pain?" As stated, it is my contention that if you have ever writhed with pain or fear then you are capable of dancing before the Lord. Do you need training? Sign up. I remember as I planned a dance conference and debated the price of the fee. I agonized over charging the cost I knew we needed in order to host the conference. The Lord spoke to me and said, "Margaret, people pay for what they want." Then, He brought to my mind Disney World's admittance fee and the cost of the foods. People pay for what they want. Hmmm!

God desires that we worship Him. He desires that we give Him our all. Jesus openly (publicly) gave His life for you. **WILL YOU DANCE FOR HIM?**

**There is no greater joy in ministry than to experience the awesome presence of the Holy Spirit as you become fully engulfed in His presence. Dancing before the Lord is indeed an honor, a privilege, and a joy.**

**IT'S TIME TO DANCE (Ecclesiastes 3:4)!!!!!!!!!!!!**

1.  Taken from *Abingdon's Strong's Exhaustive Concordance Of The Bible*

# CHAPTER 7

## Personal Testimony

### The birth of a dream . . .

As a small child growing up in the sixties in a southern, rural, segregated town to parents of modest means and six children, I had little hope of receiving dance training. My earliest recollection of dancing included my parents calling the children out to dance before friends and relatives. As we twitched and jived, we would energetically display our renditions to the beat. After receiving the quarters given, we would scurry to our rooms with our newly found wealth. I remember wanting training badly, but knowing that feeding a family was more important to my father than a little dancing girl. I remember getting the encyclopedia and memorizing the basic positions of the feet and arms for ballet by reading the instructions and imitating the pictures. I vowed in my heart that one day I would dance.

### The unfolding of a dream . . .

Still, I would welcome opportunities to exhibit what I knew to be a promising talent. My oldest brother, Bennie Jr. would proudly display me to his friends. "Come here, Margaret, show them how you can stand on your toes." "See, see, I told you," he would exclaim as I balanced on the tip of my shoes, wondering if this was how the real ballerinas did it. In third grade, I recall being a part of Mrs. Dortch's dance group, but do not recall all we did. My earliest choreography memory occurred in the eighth grade with my choreography of the song, "Fall On Your Knees." Two other girls had consented to dance with me, allowing me to choreograph the dance, carving their body shapes and movements through space.

Finally, in the early seventies, I was accepted at the University of North Carolina at Chapel Hill as an undergraduate. I remember having earned the reputation of being one of the best dancers at Carolina as I and my partner, Larry Edwards, would find ourselves surrounded by people as they stood back to watch us take the dance floor. On one particular occasion, a young man asked me to dance. I said okay and followed him to the dance floor. He began a series of movements that I thought were quite strange for a party. Nevertheless, I "antiphonally" responded to his every move. At the end of the dance, he said, "I want you to come and join the Opeyo Dancers." The Opeyo dancers were a modern dance company on campus. "Don't you have to audition?" I asked. "You just did." Needless to say, I did join. This began my first introduction into the world of dance training. Later, as a MFA graduate student in theatre at the University of North Carolina at Chapel Hill, dance became a part of our every day training. Outdoor theatre, community theatre, and dance concerts all became my way of life . . . Until . . .

## A dream revisited . . .

In December of 1974, I accepted Christ as my Lord Savior. Having been brought up in a traditional church, I had been taught that dancing was a "sin." The only acceptable dance I saw was Mrs. C's almost weekly dance rendition (shouting) at the end of our pastor's sermon. She was predictable so everyone accepted it as being Mrs. C. Beyond that, dancing was a sin, theatre was a sin . . .

I loved the Lord and did not want to grieve Him in anyway, nor did I want to cause anyone to stumble. So, I gave it up, dancing and the theatre until . . . the Holy Spirit started ministering to me. God said, "Margaret, I did not tell you to give it up. Just give it to me. **Change the way** you do it, **change why** you do it, **and change where** you do it." **Imagine, when I read in the Word the command to "praise Him in the dance." Hallelujah!!!**

And that's what I did. There was some persecution as I began to dance before the Lord. During that time period, the churches were nowhere near as open as they are now. God placed in my life Dr. (Chap) Kenneth and Rosali Edwards of the Beulah Outreach Ministries who became spiritual parents to me. Under their leadership and guidance, I began to grow in the areas of ministry which included dance and theatre. Isn't it good to know that we can use the gifts that God has given us for HIS GLORY!

## The dream lives on . . .

I marvel at God and know He has moved in my life. He has allowed me the opportunity to teach dance in one of the most prestigious magnet school in the country, William G. Enloe High School. He has allowed me to dance with Chuck Davis of the African American Dance Ensemble in a Master class on the PBS special, *Dance In America*. He has opened doors for me to minister, dance and teach dance in and out of the country through First Congregational Church of Christ; Zina Christian Center, Beulah Outreach Ministries, A Cry For The Children Ministries, Inc., the Full Gospel Baptist Church Fellowship of NC; the International Full Gospel Baptist Church Fellowship; Baptist General Convention of Virginia; International Dance Commission-Dancing Preachers, First Shiloh Baptist Church of Virginia, etc. And later, He gave me a team, Arts-4-Christ Ministry and Mentoring Team, which mentors and prepares leaders of dance ministries. He continues to astound me. I can only praise Him for everything He has done and is doing.

As I continue to serve Him, I want to encourage you give Him your all. Accept Him as your Savior and Lord, and allow Him to lead you. There is a way that seems right unto a man (Proverbs 16:25a) but as for God His way is perfect (Psalm 18:30a). Let Him order your steps (Psalm 37:23a; Proverbs 16:9b). He knows the plans He has for your life (Jeremiah 29:11).

**It is my desire to impart in you all that He has given me, to encourage you to experience His fullness and completeness, as you minister before the Lord in dance.**

**As a leader of worship through dance, expect to be attacked. Expect to be attacked! Think it not strange! (1Peter 4:12-14).** The Word says that the thief comes but to "steal, and to kill, and to destroy" (John 10:10). The enemy does not want the Word of God to go out in any form. When you enter the realm of praise and worship, you are exacting warfare on the on the enemy's head. You are bringing other soldiers into a realm where the Lord of Host can effectively equip His army. The enemy does not want this and therefore, you will fight all kinds of battles on every front.

I recall a season when I developed severe pains in my lower back. The pains came from out of nowhere. Not even the doctors could explain what had happened. The pain became severe that I could not sit (but for only a very minutes), and could not bend over freely. The pain increased in intensity and duration to the point where, at times, I had to lie on my side in school and stand in the back of the church. This attack occurred at the time when God was launching me out further in the area of dance ministry at the conference in New Orleans, as well as, expanding in our church. As a part of the expansion, we had instituted technique classes twice a month. The Full Gospel Baptist Church Fellowship of North Carolina (FGBCF) Dance and Banner Ministry was ministering in New Orleans, preparing through rehearsals, and expanding statewide with workshops. A Cry For The Children Ministries, Inc had just begun offering three monthly praise and worship dance classes. I registered to take a weekly ballet class at one of the local dance studios, and I was writing this book.

After having consulted three doctors and a physical therapist, I was told three different things as a possible source. No one knew! I was given drugs and a referral to a specialist. But God!!! But God!!! God knew the calling on my life. God knew that He had "invested" in me. **God knew I would be able to stand.**

I began to walk by faith and not by sight. I took the medicine, the physical therapy treatments, and the exercise program. I followed the guidelines given, but I did not stop. I knew the God which I served__The Lord of Host! I knew that God would not call me in ministry and then attack me while doing it. So, I continued. At times, I typed on my knees, taught the dance classes with modifications as advised by the therapist, and traveled with a pillow at my back. God had begun a work; I knew He would finish it. I noticed that as I began to do what God had called me to do, the pain began to lessen. I am not trying to offer you advice concerning your physical conditions; I am just telling you what had happened to me. Hallelujah!!

In your dance ministry, it is imperative that you have intercessors or that you link with an intercessory ministry. I generally require each of the dancers to fast as we prepare for ministry. You may want to plan a session where your dancers come together to war in the heavenlies through prayer and fasting. At any rate, expect to be attacked, **but EXPECT A VICTORY!!!**

**WARRIORS! . . . IT'S TIME TO *PRASIE HIM IN THR DANCE!* (Ecclesiastes 3:4)**

# Appendix A

## Dance Glossary

**Adage**—(Adagio) slow, sustained movements.

**Adlib**—to allow the dancer to create dance phrases spontaneously, dance phrases not previously choreographed.

**Allegro**—lively, quick.

**Antiphonal**—an alternation of responses (call and response).

**Asymmetrical**—unbalanced picture of design.

**Axial**—Non-locomotor movements of the body around its personal space (self space, own space).

**Balance**—symmetrical in design, equal representation on both sides.

**Beat**—pulse of rhythm, song, movement.

**Choreographic notation**—(choreology) a means of recording dance movements in organized patterns and designs

**Choreography**—art of planning dance movements through a code of symbols.

**Dance composition**—arrangement of movements that create a dance,

**Dance phrase**—a sequence of organized movements with a distinct beginning and end. It can be used to create the entire dance composition.

**Diagonal**—slanted from angle to angle.

**Fine motor movements**—small muscle movements.

**General space**—the area around the stage or ministry area (pulpit) in which the movement occurs.

**Gross motor movements**—large muscle movements.

**Levels**—(elevation) high, medium, low.

**Locomotor**—movements that travel from place to place in the general space: hop, walk, skip, jump, slide, spin, twirl, turn, run, etc.

**Measure**—unit of measuring music separated by bars.

**Non-locomotor**—movements that are performed in the personal space. They can be created by the body making angular and curved shapes in the personal space.

**Personal space**—space around the individual (self space).

**Proscenium**—framework through which the stage or performance (ministry) is seen. The fourth wall concept. It is as if the stage is a box with four walls, and one wall was removed so that the audience can see.

**Round/canon**—series of overlapping movements, staggered with the beginning and ending of the dance phrase, much like singing a round. In a canon, movements merge at the end.

**Style/Genre—**

> **Ballet**—a formal stylized type of dance that creates graceful patterns of movements.
>
> **Modern**—contemporary dance that broke away from the traditions of ballet, uses parallel positions.
>
> **Jazz**—energetic syncopated movements.
>
> **Contemporary**—reflects movements of the time period.
>
> **Tap**—primarily the movement of the feet with special metal toe cap shoes.

**Symmetry**—balancing the stage space with corresponding levels and directions, poses, tableaus or movements that match on each side. If you fold the picture in half it matches.

**Tableau**—a still picturesque representation of a scene.

**Tempo**—speed (fast, slow, moderate, etc.)

**Theme**—central idea or concept, main idea.

**Transition**—(transitional phrase) (transitional movement)-movement from one tableau to another or from one area of the stage to another.

# Appendix B

## Sample Governance Structure

### Governing Structure A

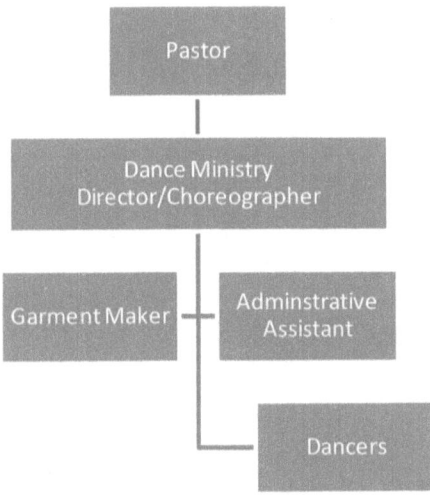

### Governing Structure B

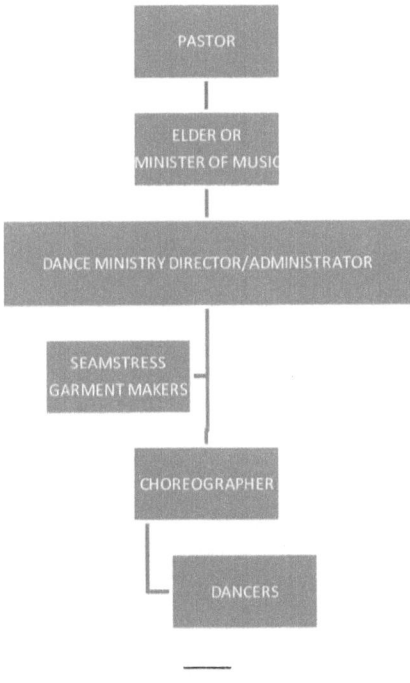

# Appendix B

## Sample Governance Structure (continued)

**Governing Structure C**

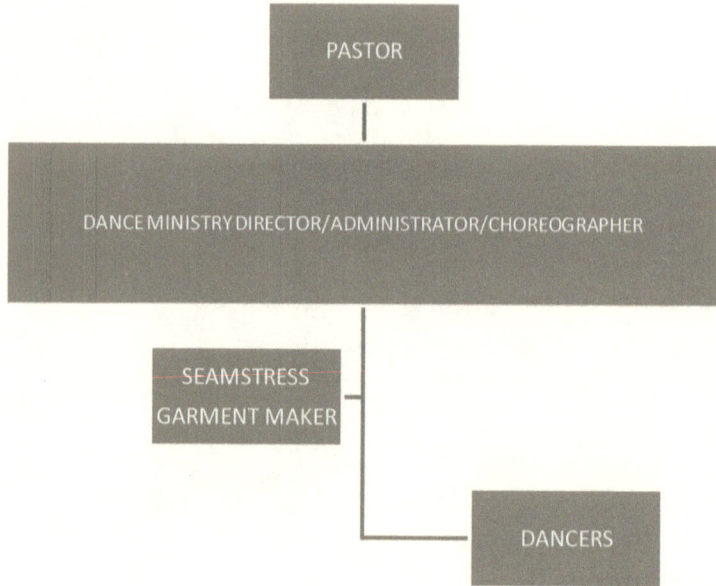

# Appendix C

## Sample Commitment Sheet: Contract or Memorandum Of Understanding Dance & Banner Ministry Guidelines

Director:      Dr. Margaret B. Wright (919) 555-1234

Asst. Director: _____

### Requirements:
Must be saved. (Dancer has accepted Jesus Christ as Lord and Savior).
**Note:** Dance is a ministry. How can someone be expected to minister before the Lord on the behalf of others and he/she does not even know the Lord.
Must be a member of church in good standing and in regular attendance.
Must be a member of covenant care (in regular attendance).
Must have previous training or evidence of talent in the area of dance.
Must have parental permission if under 18 years of age.
Must be willing to get additional training.

### Acknowledgements:
1. I understand that this is a dance ministry and not a dance performance.
2. I understand that everything will be done in agreement with the Word of God.
3. I understand that by joining I will be making a commitment to the ministry for one year, and therefore, will attend rehearsals, classes.
4. I understand that I must conduct myself in a proper manner, and follow those in authority.
5. I understand that in order to minister in dance, I must attend all rehearsals.
6. I understand that that if I must be absent from rehearsal, except in the case of emergency, I will contact in advance the necessary person, (e.g. Minister _____ at 555-1234 or Sister/Brother _____ at 555-5678).
7. I understand that I must dress appropriately to minister.
8. I understand that if my schedule changes and I am unable to faithfully attend, I may request a leave of absence for a reasonable time period (if three months or more, I may be asked to resign and reapply next year).
9. I have prayed (with parents and/or guardian, if applicable) and believe that God has called me to this ministry at this appointed time.

Participant Signature: _____ Date: _____
Parent/Guardian Signature: _____ Date: _____

_____

Received Confirmation of faithful attendance from Covenant Care Leader: ___Yes ___No
Leader _____ Date _____

---

# Appendix D

**Dance Ministry Tryout/Audition Or Placement Guide**

Name: _____ Age (If Under 18): _____

Address: _____

Home Phone Number: _____ Email Address: _____

_____

Parent's/Guardian's Name (If Applicable):_____

Parent's Email Address: _____

**PLACEMENT: ___ CHILDREN ___YOUTH_____ADULT _____ APPRENTICE**
**_____ DANCE COMPANY**

| Ratings: Use Scale 1-5 | 1-Poor | 2-Fair | 3-Good | 4-Very Good | 5-Proficient |
|---|---|---|---|---|---|
| **Interest** | | | | | |
| Interest/Willingness (Responds to corrections) | | | | | |
| Effort (Works hard) | | | | | |
| Attentive to directions | | | | | |
| | | | | | |
| **Creativity** | | | | | |
| Inventive/Creative ability to improvise | | | | | |
| Form (Uses body to create shapes & movement) | | | | | |
| Choreographic abilities | | | | | |
| | | | | | |
| **Skills/Ability Levels (Dance Form)** | | | | | |
| Responds to accompaniment (Music-Sound) | | | | | |
| Aligns properly-Evidence of technique | | | | | |
| Extends foot/leg | | | | | |
| Maintains proper arms positions | | | | | |
| Correlates movements to the type of song | | | | | |
| Executes movements properly (locomotor) | | | | | |
| Executes movements properly (non-locomotor) | | | | | |
| Works well as an ensemble | | | | | |
| | | | | | |
| **Spiritual Commitment** | | | | | |
| Expresses a commitment to Christ | | | | | |
| Demonstrates a heart for dancing | | | | | |
| Total Score | | | | | |

## Strengths:

## Weaknesses:

## Additional Comments:

# Appendix E

Sample Worship Diary

**Week: 1**        **Day 1** *Mon. June 1, 1999*

**Dance Word and definitions:** *Raqad*-raw-kad'
(Job 21:11; Ec. 3:4; Is. 13:21; 1 Chron. 15:29). The word for the dance means to stamp, i.e. to spring about widely or joyfully."

**Music Selected** "Jesus is Real" by One Accord

**Movements Used:** I began with stamping (marching around the room). Later, I started jumping and hopping.

**God's Word to Me:** No spoken word today, but the Lord filled me with such joy as I danced in His presence that I fell on the floor while laughing.

**About the experience:** I felt kind of awkward at first, like I was in the military. Later, I thought I must have looked like a child on the playground. It was kind of fun, but I am glad no one could see me.

# Appendix F

## Selected Bibliography

*American heritage dictionary.* (Standard ed.). CD-ROM. Boston: Houghton Mifflin.

Burton, W., & Burton, J. (1996). *Covenant care group: A guide to establishing a church cell group ministry.* Raleigh: Waymond & Jacquelyn Burton Ministries, Inc.

Burton, Jr. W. L. (1999). *Managing god's finances.* Raleigh: Waymond & Jacquelyn Burton Ministries, Inc.

Dennis, J. A. *The holy spirit.* Austin: Words of Life, Inc.

Foster, R. D. *Seven minutes with god: How to plan a daily quiet time.* Colorado Springs: Navpress.

Frazier, D. (1999). *Send for me a minstrel.* Brooklyn: God's Music Incorporated Publishing.

Hagin, K. E. (1984). *The precious blood of Jesus.* Tulsa: Rhema Bible Church.

Hagin, Jr. K. (1983). *Get acquainted with God.* Tulsa: Rhema Bible Church.

Lockhart, A. S. (1977). *Modern dance: Building and teaching lessons.* (5th ed.). Dubuque: Wm. C. Brown Publishing Company

Minton, S. C. (1986). *Choreography: A basic approach using improvisation.* Champaign: Human Kinetics Publishers.

Munger, R. B. (1954). *My heart Christ's home.* Downers Grove: Inter-Varsity Christian Fellowship of the United States of America.

Penrod, J., & Plastino, J. G. (1980). (2nd ed.). *The dancer prepares. Modern dance for beginners.* Palo Alto: Mayfield Publishing Company.

Smith, L. (1991). *Usborne guide: Dance.* Tulsa: EDC Publishing.

Strong, J. (1980). *Abingdon's strong's exhaustive concordance of the bible.* Madison: Abingdon.

Vine, W. E., Unger, M. F., & White, Jr. W. (1980). *Vine's complete expository dictionary of old and new testament words.* Nashville: Thomas Nelson, Inc.

# Appendix G

## About A Cry for the Children, Inc.

**For the vision is yet for an appointed time, But at the end it will speak, and it will not lie. Through it tarries, wait for it; Because it will surely come, It will not tarry (Habakkuk 2:3).**

## About The Vision:

In the late 1970's after my conversion experience, I had a dream. As the dream opened, I was approaching a large two story white house. I had been hired as a teacher to teach children who "for some reason" had been kicked out of public schools. As I entered the doorway, I was greeted by a large white person with long white hair dressed in a long white robe. (I could not tell whether the person was a male or female. He appeared to be male.) He pointed into a room and left to go down a narrow hallway. Entering the room, I discovered children about middle school age fighting and creating havoc. In other words, they were "turning the place out." I asked the Lord what to do. He said, "Positive reinforcement." I understood what that meant. I had used the technique as a part of a behavior modification program, while working in a mental institution. As I began to use various techniques incorporating positive reinforcement, the children began to settle down and started to learn. Soon, everything was in order.

Suddenly, two adults entered the room (male and female). They seemed unaware that we were in the room and began to kiss and fondle each other as they moved towards the chairs to sit, continuing their actions. The children began to notice and started giggling and imitating the adults' behavior. Immediately, an older lady came in carrying a bible and falling over chairs and children while yelling, "Hallelujah, Glory to God?" She began to gyrate and twitch, as if under the influence of a spirit. I tried to tell the adults to get out and that this was no place for such behavior.

The children went wild, some imitating the religious woman and the others imitating the couple making out. I left the room and ran down the hall to find the person that had hired me to tell him that if he would come and remove the adults, I could teach the children. As I entered an opened doorway, I found the white figure sitting on a commode with his foot propped on the bathtub, nonchalantly smoking a cigarette. Before I could open my mouth to speak, my eyes were drawn to my right. Three small children, about four or five years old, were floating face down in the bathtub, drowning.

Frantically, one by one, I grabbed each child and tried to pull him over the side of the bathtub. As soon as I would release one to grab another, the first would slip back into the tub. I cried, "Lord, what shall I do?" The Lord replied,

"Cut the source." I then noticed that the water was pouring from a faucet and running over the edge of the tub. I turned off the faucet, and the water in the tub began to go down the drain. Then, I was able to grab each child and lay him across the edge of the tube. Ferverently, I began patting each child on his backs. The children began to cough and out their mouths came water, blood, cigarette butts, crushed beer cans and other trash. Crying, I asked the Lord, "Will these be saved?" He replied, "These will because they are young, but what about the others in that room?" I woke up.

**Birthing the Vision:**

**A**_An alarming number of children are succumbing to drugs, violence, sex and suicide; they are dying without Christ in their lives.

**C**_Children are our most valuable assets.

**F**_Fortifying our children with the Word of God is the only hope. We seek to strengthen our youth by proclaiming the gospel through visual and performing arts (theatre arts, dance, music) and sign language; thus, building mighty warriors for Christ.

**C**_Christ is the only answer.

**A Cry for the Children, Inc.'s (ACFC, Inc.)** vision is to evangelize every child in the world through the arts.

**ACFC, Inc.** is a Spirit led, Word fed multimedia ministry whose mission is to teach biblical principles through the use of the creative arts (visual, performing, media, and sign language) and to assist churches, para-churches, organizations, and other ministries in establishing creative ministries, within their entity, as tools for building and sustaining ministry with youth and children.

> The Spirit of the Lord God is upon Me, because the Lord has anointed Me to preach good tidings to the poor; He has sent Me to heal the brokenhearted, To proclaim liberty to the captives, And the opening of the prison to those who are bound; To proclaim the acceptable year of the Lord, And the day of the vengeance of our God; To comfort all who mourn, To console those who mourn in Zion, To give them beauty for ashes, the oil of joy for mourning, The garment of praise for the spirit of heaviness; that they may be called the tree of righteousness, The planting of the Lord, that he may be glorified. And they shall raise up former desolations, and they shall repair the ruined cities, the desolations of many generations (Isaiah 61:1-4).

**ACFC, Inc. will:**

1) Teach Biblical principles that will enhance the quality of life of all participants;

2) Assist churches, para-churches, organizations, and other ministries in establishing the visual and performing arts sign language and other creative ministries, within their structure, as tools for building and sustaining ministry with youth and children;

3) Use creative tools for evangelizing youth and children, especially from unchurched backgrounds and communities;

4) Establish educational programs and community outreaches that promote healthy assets for children and youth development;

5) Establish a team that will travel internationally teaching and preaching the Word of God and presenting the gospel of Jesus Christ through the arts (visual, performing and media, inclusive of music, theatre arts, and dance) and sign language;

6) Include other entities as part of our primary entity which includes establishing satellite operations or extended facilities in different locations.

**Fulfilling the Vision:**

In September of 2014 I had a vision. As the vision opened, I was standing in a grassy meadow facing Jesus who was standing on a hill, clothed in His majesty with a long flowing robe. All of sudden children came from the left, right, and from behind me running towards Jesus on the hill. The children surrounded Jesus and began to jump up and down, while laughing. I found myself in the crowd with the children, joyfully jumping with Jesus. All at once, a few of the children from the left and right began to soar up in the air flying towards the four corners of the earth. The other children continued to joyfully jump with Jesus. As I found myself back in the grassy field facing the scene, Jesus opened His robe and said, "It's time for the children to come in." Children coming from every direction ran towards Jesus going into Him through the opening in the robe, some running, some walking, some crawling, and some dragging a leg. As the last child entered, He closed His robe and soared to heaven.

"IT'S TIME FOR THE CHILDRENTO COME IN."

# APPENDIX H
## About the Author
## Dr. Margaret Brewington [Douglass] Wright

Margaret, an ordained and commissioned apostle, is called to restore peoples' hearts to God for worship through the arts. Margaret has extensive experience (over 40 year) in using the arts for ministerial outreach and education. She has developed and conducted liturgical, modern dance and African dance classes for various organizations, community centers, churches, and public schools. In addition to a Bachelor of Art and Master of Fine Arts in Theatre from the University of North Carolina, Chapel Hill; she also holds a Master of School Administration and a PhD in Educational Research and Policy Analysis with a minor in curriculum and instruction and from North Carolina State University. Her dissertation: *Professional Artists as Teachers with At-risk Youth: A Narrative Case Study*. She is a graduate of the Certificate in Theology program from the Interdenominational Theological Seminary in Atlanta Georgia; the Formational Prayer certificate program from Ashland Theological Seminary in Ashland, Ohio; and the School of Prophets from The Apostolic Prophetic Connection under Apostle Dr. Elizabeth Hairston McBurrows.

Margaret, an enthusiast for the arts, has served for over four decades in a myriad of roles: actress, dancer, singer, choreographer, director, playwright, poet, author, education consultant, public school teacher (theatre, English, dance, and gifted education); rehabilitation therapist using dance and drama as a therapeutic tool with psychiatric and intellectually challenged adults; instructor Dabney S. Lancaster Community College in Clifton Forge, Virginia and Meredith College in Raleigh, North Carolina (Theatre and Speech); school principal in Virginia Commonwealth University's hospital education program, a mental health hospital in NC, and a juvenile correctional facility in VA. In addition to holding certifications in teaching English, Dance and Theatre in Virginia and North Carolina, she also holds licensures as a Principal/School Administrator (NC, VA, LA) and Division Superintendent (VA and LA). As a performing artist, Margaret appeared with the Playmakers Repertory Company, The Liberty Cart Outdoor Theatre, and community theatre. While at UNC-CH, she wrote, directed and performed in a play for evangelistic outreach called *Tell Them I Love Them*. She danced in the PBS special, "Dance in America" with the internationally renowned Chuck Davis of the Africa American Dance Ensemble and performed a one-woman dinner theatre production at Dabney S. Lancaster Community College.

Heeding a call to ministry, Margaret traveled with Beulah Outreach Ministries of Siler City, N. C. using the arts to present the gospel. She founded A Cry for the Children (ACFC) in 1997 and later Creative Arts Institute of Diversified Learning, both non-profit organizations that use the arts as a powerful tool for instruction and outreach. She is the founder/director of ACFC, Inc's Arts-4-Christ Ministry & Mentoring Team whose mission is to "equip" the body of Christ for the work of the ministry (Eph. 4:11-16)" using the arts by providing foundational and ongoing assistance in establishing, developing and strengthening ministries through an arts leaders' mentoring institutes, workshops and seminars. She served as an associate minister of Creative Arts for First Shiloh Baptist Church of Mechanicsville, Virginia; director of NC Full Gospel Baptist Church Fellowship Dance and Banner Ministry and the Virginia State Coordinator for the International Dance Commission. Margaret is the author of three books: *Dancing In His Presence: A Guide to Establishing and Maintaining a Dance Ministry* (book, workbook and Instructor's manual). She has assisted numerous churches in establishing creative arts ministries: dance, theatre, and puppetry. Through ACFC, she implemented the Arts-4-Christ conferences. Later, she established an educational outreach to West Africa, "Students & Educators Celebrating Diversity" for three summers in West Africa: Ghana (1997, 1998, & 2000) and Benin (2000). The outreach was designed to promote an understanding of the mores and customs of West Africa and to provide a historical and cultural link to African American history. As a result, she appeared in a BBC documentary with Harvard University's Professor, Dr. Henry Louis Gates Jr. Additionally, each year, the participants were able to witness and participate in dance with a professional company, e.g. KoKrobeti School of drumming and dancing, University of Ghana at Legon, etc.

Margaret, a wife, mother of four, grandmother of eight, and great-grandmother of two **adores the Lord and gives her all for His Glory!**

# Appendix I

## Creative Arts Resources

**Services**
**Arts-4-Christ Ministry and Mentoring Team**

**Who are we?** Arts-4-Christ Ministry & Mentoring Team is a coalition of Christian ministers and professional artists, a committed group of worshipers, whose mission is to "equip" the body of Christ for the work of the ministry (Eph. 4:11-16) using the arts by providing foundational and ongoing assistance in establishing, developing or strengthening ministries through evangelistic outreach, workshops, seminars, arts leaders' mentoring institutes. Birthed out of the A Cry for the Children Minstries' Arts-4-Christ Conferences, the TEAM forwards the vision by helping churches and ministries establish ministry through the arts for Christ: Levitical Worship; Evangelistic Outreach; Banners and Flags; Garments and Worship Props; Choreography for Praise and Worship; Dance Technique (Liturgical, African, Modern, Pageantry); Music for Praise and Worship; Theatre Arts: Play Production, Readers Theatre, Scripting Writing, Creative Dramatics, Mime, Acting, Puppetry, Spoken Word, Script Writing.

For information about training, mentoring, and ministry events send email to dancinginhispresence@gmail.com.

**Training/Workshops**
**Arts-4-Christ Dancing In His Presence Dance Leader's Mentoring Institute: Certificate Program for Leaders of Dance Ministry**

DIHP-Dance Leaders Mentoring Institute is a foundational *"must"* for dance leaders. The Institute provides three levels of mentoring for leaders that incorporates biblical foundation, operational and administrative structure, vision, mission, budget, Levitical praise and worship, dance movements selection, choreography, garments, banners, flags, worship props, pageantry, music selection for praise & worship, criteria for dance leaders and dancers, intercessory prayer team, role of the worshipper, pastor/leader relationship, etc. Training includes monthly teleconference, workshops, seminars, guest speakers and ministry opportunities. Certification is available for dance leaders who complete the three leveled institute.

## Drama/Theatre Training Institute

Drama/Theatre for ministry training sessions are available in the following areas: acting, directing, plays or skits for liturgical worship, play production, script writing, creative drama, puppetry, Spoken Word, Reader's Theatre, and Mime.

## PRODUCTS BOOKS: Dancing in His Presence Book Series

**Dance Leader's Instructor's Manual:** *Dancing In His Presence: A Guide to Establishing and Maintaining a Dance Ministry Instructor's Manual* (Includes sample forms and templates on CD)

**Workbook:** *Dancing In His Presence: A Guide to Establishing and Maintaining a Dance Ministry Workbook*

**Book:** *Dancing In His Presence: A Guide to Establishing and Maintaining a Dance Ministry* (1999)1st Edition

**Dance Leader's Ministry Packet CD** (Contains sample forms and templates for organizing and governing dance ministries)

For information about additional publications or to order the DIHP product series email dancinginhispresence@gmail.com

**We, the Arts-4-Christ Ministry and Mentoring Team, are excited about the Mentoring Institute Certificate Program in Arts Ministry.** As mentors in the use of the arts as a form of worship, we take seriously a mandate given to us by God, "Don't let them misrepresent me!" Therefore, as a critical part of our calling, we offer training sessions to ensure that you gain a biblical foundation in ministry, as well as, instructional strategies for imparting into others the skills that you have learned. As, you begin your journey in arts ministry, preparation is a critical part of that process. **We look forward to serving you through the Institutes.**

www.ingramcontent.com/pod-product-compliance
Lightning Source LLC
Chambersburg PA
CBHW021007180526
45163CB00005B/1924